Parenting for a healthy future

Dotty T. Coplen

Hawthorn Press

Parenting for a Healthy Future © 1995 Dotty Coplen
Published by Hawthorn Press, Hawthorn House, 1, Lansdown Lane,
Stroud, Gloucestershire, GL5 1BJ, U.K. Fax (01453) 751138

First Edition
Cover picture design by Ivon Oates
Typeset by Qwertyop 01453 766716
Printed in Great Britain

British Library Cataloguing in Publicaton Date applied for.

ISBN 1 869 890 53 1

Contents

Introduction:
Understanding the Task 3
      Changing Needs; Artful Parenting; Protecting the
      Child; Seeing the Whole; Knowing Your Goals

Chapter 1:
Finding the Way 9
      Understanding Spoiling; Defining the Issues; In
      Simpler Times; Our Invisible Times; Families Apart;
      Beyond Common Sense

Chapter 2:
Knowing the Child 15
      Meeting the Inner Reality; The Inner Wisdom;
      Machines Can't Grow; Animal Instincts; Uniquely
      Human Qualities

Chapter 3:
Allowing Humanness 21
      Human Thinking; Heartfelt Thinking; Recognizing
      Feelings; Handling Negative Feelings; Allowing
      Individuality

Chapter 4:
The Child Meets the World 28
      Learning Boundaries; Guiding Interests; Rule of
      Three; Learning from the Environment; Valuing
      Harmony

Chapter 5:
Punishment or Discipline 36
      Understanding the Difference; Power Needs;
      Learning Respect; Social Consciousness; Behaviour is
      Learned

Chapter 6:
From Discipline to Self Discipline 42
      Learning Healthy Choices; Finding Balance; Social
      Learning; Personal Values; Sharing with Others

Chapter 7:
Learning Values 49
      Taking Responsibility; Resolving Conflict; Checking
      the Rules; Family Rules; Making Right Choices

iv

Chapter 8:
Image or Reality **56**
> Caring for Things; Valuing Nature; Looking Beyond Image; Seeking Inner Reality; Cooperation from Caring

Chapter 9:
Nature, Needs and Humanness **62**
> Knowing the Whole Person; Need or Want; Understanding Nature and Needs; Developing Trust; Setting Limits; Need for Acceptance

Chapter 10:
Learning for Harmony **72**
> Society's Ways; Observation; Realistic Expectations; Self Esteem; Solving Problems

Chapter 11:
Affirming the Child **79**
> Notice Me Please; Sharing Tasks; Building Self Confidence

Chapter 12:
Calm Mealtimes **84**
> Physiological/Psychological Needs; Personal Likes and Dislikes; Avoid Eating Wars; Presenting Healthy Food; The Pitfalls are Many; Eating with Gratitude; Avoiding Rewarding with Sweets; Enjoying Eating

Chapter 13:
Happy Bedtimes **95**
> The Need for Ritual; The Miracle of Sleep; Relaxing in Comfort; Transition to Sleep; Value of Ritual; Fear of the Dark; Bedtime Problems

Chapter 14:
Listening to your child **104**
> Communication Through Words; Communication Through Listening; "I" Messages; Understanding Through Words; Excuse Me Please; Different Views

Chapter 15:
Growing Socially 115
Practising for Life; The Value of Rules; Experiencing
Differences; Enjoy the Experience; Fair Play; The
Urge to Grow

Chapter 16:
The World We Live In 122
Seeking Values; Becoming Aware; Human Qualities;
Honouring Others

The author wishes to point out that she has deliberately chosen to alternate masculine and feminine pronouns in succeeding chapters.

Introduction

Understanding the task

Welcome to the mysterious world of Childhood. What an amazing part of life it is, from the enchanting smile of an infant to her frustrating restless fretting. Who is this little one and how can we get to know her, learn how to care for her, and relate to this time of magic? We know that we want the best for her, but we find it difficult to know what that "best" is.

We sense that being a parent is one of life's most important tasks but how do we give it that priority in our lives? In general there is little training for the job and not enough understanding of the basic purpose of the task at hand.

Changing Needs

How can parents sort out what the child needs? How can they know what their goal is as parents? Finding the short term goal may not be so difficult: we want to get things back on track, to end any conflict or uncertainty. The long term goal may be less clear. There is today, there is also tomorrow. Today we have a child; after many tomorrows we will have an adult. What is needed now? What will also be needed between now and then?

A baby's life begins with the parents having total responsibility for the care and protection for the child. Parents hope that after about eighteen years of childhood, all the responsibilities can be given over to the young adult. It will be an ever changing process over time. The challenge is to understand that the requirements are many and that these requirements change over time.

What an infant needs is different from what a first grader needs and that is different from what an adolescent needs. This requires that the parent has the necessary skills and qualities needed to care for the totally dependent infant-toddler and can also be a role model for the child to learn from as she grows.

The child needs help in learning life's skills and developing the human qualities needed for life. After learning the skills she will need space to allow her to practise them herself. Ideally, that space will be allowed without criticism. The qualities that allow a young adult to live a fruitful life are built up in many small steps, one after the other.

Parents face the challenge of being able to move from taking total responsibility for the child to allowing the child to learn to do things for herself. Giving the child the opportunity to do what she is capable of when the abilty is sufficiently developed takes real objective judgment on the part of the parent, as well as an intimate awareness of the child. The parent has to be able to change as the needs of the child change; the parent also has to grow.

Artful Parenting

In helping the child to learn life's skills and then practise those skills, later allowing her to take over the direction of her own life, parenting becomes an art, neither asking too soon, nor delaying too long. There is no formula or recipe, but parents must be aware of the child and in tune with her needs and abilities. It is a dance, not a science experiment. Parent-child conflicts usually occur during the transition from directions coming from the parent to the child, to the child being inner directed, developing self direction and self control.

The child's task is the opposite of the parent's task. The child has the awesome task of growing from the total dependence of an infant to the self dependence of an adult. Children need to learn how to use and take care of their bodies, how to interact with others, how to work in the world, how to recognize and understand their own feelings and respect the feelings of others. All these and more are the tasks of childhood.

The nature of growth and development means that children change daily. There are also changes brought about by learning from life experiences in their environment. Children learn from their environment. The selection and creation of a healthy environment for your child is another parental responsibility.

Protecting The Child

Childhood is a profound word that can roll off our tongue without our really thinking about its meaning. Understanding that word can help us with our parenting goals. The first part of the word, **child**, describes a visible person, but what about **hood?** Hood is a protective covering, something that protects what is inside. Childhood is the time when the inner developing individuality of the person needs to be protected so that she can later realize her own humanness. The wisdom of nature has given about fourteen years for the physical maturing and learning about living life on earth. And the wisdom of society has given another seven years to learn to make healthy choices, and gain social, ethical and moral maturity. Parents need to recognize the deep significance of childhood and care for it wisely, assure that it is protected when needed and allow the child to live in the world when she is able. The importance of the parents during these years of childhood is immense.

All this requires a lot from parents and seems to require a crash course on parenting. If you can find the time, it is off to the bookstore for a "how to" book. After reading a few of these books, parents have a new problem, that is deciding which one to believe and follow!

Books do not give consistent advice. Not only is there disagreement on how to parent, but it is no longer clear what a parent's role is, nor what is right. Right for whom: right for the parent, right for the child, or right for the society? One book will say, "pick up the baby when she cries". Another book says, "don't spoil the baby by picking her up when she cries". Now which is it? Clearly, you can learn to do either one, but you cannot follow both when they are contradictory. The problem of what to do is replaced by the dilemma of deciding what to believe. Which is right?

Before the books, parents just did what they remembered their parents doing, or followed their own instincts. Now parents are also faced with the ideas of professionals and experts. Books and magazines may provide new concepts for parents without providing any understanding of what the long term effects of the advice will be.

Seeing The Whole

Human actions carry with them an intent or purpose even though we are not always aware of the purpose or intentions of the act. Sometimes it is a subconscious intention, and sometimes it is the intention of another or others that we carry out. There is a purpose to every action or we would not be doing it. The more we understand about the future consequences of what we are doing, and the intent that goes with the action, the more successful we will be in caring for our children with our own purposes and goals of parenting in mind.

Parents need to decide *together* what they believe to be a healthy human being. Then they can define their own goals in guiding their child through childhood to becoming a healthy mature citizen of the world. Parents also need to recognize how important they are in their child's daily learning and social development. The importance of parents as role models for their children to imitate cannot be overstated.

Knowing Your Goals

In order for parenting to be a conscious art, some understanding of child development is necessary, an idea of how behaviour is learned and some concepts of what a healthy human being is. It is important to recognize that, in healthy living, plans or goals come before actions. Think before you act.

If you are making bread or a cake or cookies you will use many of the same ingredients, but in differing proportions. You first decide what you are going to make, and then you select a recipe. You choose directions after deciding what you want to create. You first choose your outcome, then you follow appropriate directions to achieve that goal. You do not stir together ingredients and then wait to see what it is after you have baked it. You plan ahead. You start with a clear intention.

The experience of carefully and intentionally combining separate ingredients and enjoying what you have created is a pleasant one. Unfortunately, we have lost many of the opportunities for creativeness that our grandparents had. When you buy bread and cookies made by someone else or you make them from a mix, you have unwittingly let our world of technology short change you of a meaningful human experience. You will not have had the opportunity to experience your part in creating something new. Creating something new helps us to understand the relationship of the parts to the whole and to experience subtle differences and variations.

Gardening is one life experience that helps us to be aware of creation and growth, but that too is removed from many lives today. Seeds would not be planted without knowing what the seeds would produce; if a gardener wanted to have a vegetable garden and planted flower seeds he would be disappointed at harvest time to find that he had a garden of flowers. In gardening we know we have to plant the seeds of what we later want to harvest. In parenting, too, we need to plant the seeds for healthy humanness. We need to know the consequences of what we are doing.

By exploring the development of humanness, it is my hope that you will have the basis for being the parents that you choose to be. Knowing the principles of human behaviour, understanding basic human needs, observing developmental stages in childhood while celebrating humanness, parents can be helped with their role in the development of their children.

This is a book for parents who want to understand and grow in humanness; for parents who recognize that what happens in the world does matter and that what they do as parents will influence the future of their children, their own future, and that of society.

Chapter 1

Finding the way

There are times of sheer delight and magic when caring for a contented infant who is overflowing with light and love. Then parenting seems like a treat and not something we need to think about, analyze or understand. Love given equals love received. It seems a natural joy of life.

Understanding spoiling

But then Auntie may come for a visit, see the loving attention that the baby is being given and pronounce: "You are spoiling that child". You begin to doubt yourself and wonder, "Am I?" Or you might say with a certain sense of pride, "I know I spoil him" when you see that as a desirable and selfless thing to do. "Spoil" has become a word with confused, unclear meaning; a double edged word and one that parents really need to be clear about.

"Being spoiled" has a negative and an envious connotation. To some it means a parent who is so giving and generous that he indulges the child's every want. To others it means a child who is demanding and unpleasant to be around; a child who is selfish and inconsiderate of others, only caring about his own needs with no consideration of others. One meaning implies a generous, selfless, giving parent and the other implies a demanding, taking child. Can we give too much? Most of us have been taught that giving is good and wanting is bad. "It is better to give than to receive".

Let us look at the meaning of "spoiled" in a broader context. When something is spoiled, it is damaged. Spoiled fruit is damaged and if sufficiently spoiled it is not edible. When you spoil something you are making, you have damaged it and it is not what you intended, not up to your expectations. A really spoiled child may be similarly damaged. Such a child is selfish, demanding, self-centred and inconsiderate. The parent may feel good about his selfless, unlimited giving to the child, but it is also important to be aware of what the child is feeling and learning. Is he learning about healthy relationships with others? Or is he learning that he is the only person who matters and so deserves to have anything he wants in this world, no matter how it affects others?

When a child is loved, cared for, protected and his basic needs met, he is not being damaged. A hungry child needs to be fed, a cold child needs to be warmed, a lonely or frightened child needs to be comforted. He needs to learn the comfort of feeling nurtured, warm and protected. Only then can he return his gift of trust. A child needs to receive care to allow him to grow into a healthy caring adult. It is when a child feels omnipotent that the world has tilted too far in his direction. A child who has felt cared for by others learns about caring, then he becomes able to care for others. In learning about caring he learns about an important part of love and humanness.

When you are faced with doubts about how you are caring for your child, ask yourself: "Am I damaging him?", "What is he learning?" Confidence in yourself and in what you are doing comes from knowing what questions to sort through and then how to find your answers.

Defining the issues

A popular book on parenting *You're a Better Parent Than You Think!** is dedicated to parents' mental health. It aims at restoring parents', confidence in themselves and allowing them to feel good about what they are doing. It is a popular theme for many people: "Don't worry, no problem, everything is fine". Being confident is important if it is based on reality, when it comes from knowing and understanding what you are doing and why. Being told not to worry without understanding what is happening is not enough. You need to know the short and long term consequences. If there is a problem you need to solve it; not worry about it but solve it.

*Guarendi, Reymond N. *You're a Better Parent Than You Think!* Prentice Hall, New Jersey, 1985

If everything was all right, parents would probably not be looking for books to buy on parenting. Guarendi's book wisely states that a relaxed parent is a better parent. It then encourages parents to use their own common sense. The problem is, what is common sense? What I sense and what you sense may not be in common.

In simpler times

When the world was less sophisticated common sense told parents, "Don't send a boy to do a man's job". Common sense told them that there was much to learn in the world. One way to learn was to be an apprentice to an experienced person. There was a dignity in learning and it was all right not to know. You could not know how to shoe a horse until you learned about shoes and horses from an experienced person. Often we forget that children have so much to learn and that they don't necessarily know something just because we think that "they are old enough to know that". They can only know what they have had the opportunity to learn.

In earlier times children daily saw what needed to be done. They worked with their parents planting the crops they needed for themselves and the animals. They learned to make necessary tools working with their parents. They helped in the care of the animals and the equipment. They watched neighbours helping neighbours. What they needed to learn to be a successful adult went on around them and they were involved in it. It was self evident, common sense, people saw it and knew it in common. You couldn't escape the experience. Families worked together in their homes and on their land, children knew they were a necessary part of the whole and could experience the value of their contribution to the family.

They didn't necessarily enjoy it, but they saw the evidence of their contribution. They could see the animals and the land needed to be cared for to provide for the families' needs. They could see that it took many hands working together. There were things that had to be done at home that could not get done if the people were not there. They had to be there and work together if they were going to have food to eat. That was common sense to them.

Our invisible times

Now it is not so clear. Few of us were encouraged to use our senses as we were growing up. Learning from observation and experience became secondary to deferring to the dictates of science and the words of authorities. In fact, most of us no longer need to use our senses in that way in our daily life.

In the move from the country to the city people's experiences changed. Parents worked for money away from home and money bought what was needed. Money became more important, learning from home experiences less so. There was less connection between people's needs and what went into meeting those needs. It became easy to believe that if you had money you could buy it. The people that made that possible became invisible. The people that needed the food or tools became invisible to the farmer and the tool maker. It is not easy to maintain appreciation for someone who is invisible, so with the separation and detachment came indifference of individuals to each other.

Now our milk usually comes from cartons, not from our own cow. Our carrots come from the market in plastic bags, not from our garden. Many children do not experience the wonder of food coming from seeds planted in freshly tilled soil. They miss the joy of seeing seeds sprout, grow into plants and then delighting in the harvest. In gardens we live with the wonders and mysteries of nature. Living knowledge comes from experience. Without such experience we risk replacing living thoughts with dead thoughts. We have the chance to actually meet and recognize the birds and bugs, plants and animals in the garden and observe how they are all connected and interact.

In gardens we have the opportunity of seeing visible life and how it is all connected in the cycles of life. That is very different from memorizing classifications of plants, animals, and insects.

Farmers valued rain as a gift from the wisdom of nature that was needed for life. Now the TV Weather Man tells us, "Sorry I can't bring you a good day today; we are going to have rain". Inevitably some children will believe it when they hear this. They will believe that the weather man really does bring the weather. He said that he did. They might also wonder why he would want to bring about a "bad day". Children do try to learn about and understand the world, but that becomes more and more difficult for them. Not only is understanding the world around us more difficult, but there are subtle changes in our way of looking at natural events. Gratitude for rain has been replaced with "don't rain on my parade".

Families apart

Rural life was immeasurably different from current life, especially life in the cities. Today the children are off to school, perhaps leaving after their parents have left for work. If the parents are working they do not have the opportunity to get to know their child's school and the teachers – teachers with whom their children spend a large part of their day learning about life. Generally, parents do not know precisely what is being taught in school; even when they do, they may not feel comfortable evaluating what is going on at school. The schools have their own guidelines. Parents are cut off from a very significant portion of their child's daily life.

Parents have less and less time with their children. This makes it more and more difficult for children to learn from their parents and more and more difficult for parents to know their child intimately. None the less, the child continues to learn from the world around him, and his personality and values are formed out of the sum total of his life's experiences.

If both parents work the house is left alone, empty. Parents are away earning the money to pay for their dream house, dream car, and the labour saving devices that they need because they are off working. The machines are at home and the people are away earning money to pay for the machines and home that they are away from. Often the child comes home to an empty house or goes to someone else's house after school. How does this tie in with the need for childhood to be protective?

Beyond common sense

The family has not had any experiences in common throughout the day. Each has been invisible to the others. When everyone returns they try to reconnect but it is not always easy to bridge a whole day of separateness. Families have not had common experiences and common thoughts during the day. Many families deal with this uneasiness by asking, "How was your day?" or "What did you do in school today?" The answer is often "fine" or "nothing". The reality is, talking about experiences is not the same as experiencing them. For those who do reconnect they do it by forgetting where they have been. They disconnect from their own day time experience and make it invisible to themselves.

No wonder parenting and family life are perplexing. It is difficult to know and understand each other when you are not spending much time together nor doing things together. Everyone seems to have too much to do, and often our own basic needs have not been met during the day. How can we come to know each other and understand each other's needs in our current world? Relying on common sense does not seem to be the answer when each person in the family is in a different environment, sensing separate experiences, living different lives. Since most families do not sense in common any more there is little basis for common sense. Common sense no longer seems to be the answer. It appears reason and understanding will have to replace common sense and instincts.

To care for and educate a child in our world of separations, we need to rediscover what humanness is as well as who a child is, and what needs to happen in childhood through parenting. We need to know who we are, really are, before we can make profound life decisions.

As a parent you have taken on the responsibility for the life of another human being. This is an amazing, hopefully delightful and certainly challenging life experience. It is a responsibility that is difficult to meet without knowing what you need to do along the way.

Chapter 2

Knowing the child

What better way to discover humanness than to start at the beginning of a human life with the birth of a baby? Of course the child's development started before birth and that is another mystery to think about, but not one that is available for us to know through our own observation. For most parents the birth of their child is a miracle of nature and if they have thought about it, they feel a sense of amazement and wonder at their role in the creation of a new being. Generally parents are aware that they did not "make" the baby, but that they were the significant enablers that cooperated for a new life to come into the world. A sperm and an ovum combining to allow for a vital new being to live on earth is a process beyond comprehension to most of us.

True, laboratories can now use technology to combine ovum and sperm, but even they cannot create ovum and sperm, they rely on the wisdom and mysteries of nature for that. If we contemplate these mysteries we become ever more aware that a child is much more than we can see from the outside. We can count the toes and fingers, describe the eyes and nose and hair, but we haven't begun to be aware of the temperament and personality of the child when we describe those features. There is much more than what we can see on the outside.

Meeting the inner reality

Each child has her own feelings and needs and expresses these to us. Each child feels her own discomfort and lets us know about that too. Neither the parent nor the doctor taught her to feel or to communicate by crying, the baby was born knowing that. A baby is no empty vessel needing to be filled by us to allow it to function. We can experience that there is an inner essence or being that seeks the satisfying of bodily needs and seeks inner harmony that brings about growth and development. This essence seeks acknowledgement and nurture. The inner reality that is not physically visible is rarely fully acknowledged, but parents do come to know and love this deeper reality.

It is difficult for science to talk about the invisible in our materially oriented world; this is probably why parents do not often read about the inner reality, the **being** of their child. It is a real, though invisible part of humanness and it must exist for the child to grow and develop. The recognition and meeting with this inner reality of ourselves and others is the basis of uniquely human interactions.

Before the baby was born, she was not visible to us, but we did not question the reality of her existence even when we could not see her with our own eyes. It helps if we remind ourselves that all real things are not visible to us. We cannot see the wind, but we know that it fills sails allowing boats to glide over the water and kites to soar in the air. Our thoughts and feelings are invisible realities; they only become visible through being verbally expressed or acted out. Our words and actions express our inner thoughts and feelings. Once a child is born we quickly experience the child as a separate person who has separate needs and will need someone else to help meet those needs. That is the meaning of birth, someone new is born into the world and it is not just visible, physical substance, it is a person.

During pregnancy the child is physically protected from the outer world by being within the mother, but at birth that protection disappears and the baby is directly affected by her outer environment. Before birth what the mother ate and drank and experienced did affect the baby, but not as directly. After the birth the baby is visible to us and the environment has a direct impact on her in a new way so we need to protect her. Awareness of this need is what has led to new approaches in childbirth where the effect on the new born baby is considered. The child needs the parents to be aware of her vulnerability so they can be sensitive to her responses. She is theirs to care for and protect, not to own, an important distinction. Remembering how sensitive and vulnerable a baby is will help us with her care. Since she has not yet developed the same defenses against sense impressions that we have, she needs extra protection. She is new and impressionable; bright lights, heat, cold, noises and confusion, are stressful for her.

When a baby cries, expressing her feelings of discomfort, we do not think of her as bad, but as expressing her own helplessness. When the infant cries we need to respond out of our concerned feelings and thoughts of providing the care that we feel is needed. We feed, we rock, we change wet clothes; we respond to the infant's ability to signal us when she needs us.

The inner wisdom

We use the child's expressions of her feelings to guide us in her care. We do not have to teach our child to signal her distress, she is born with an instinctive ability to call for help. Parents need to recognize, respect and allow this natural human ability, so that it will continue to alert us. The wisdom of the child's needs is in the child, and if we can learn to read the child we have our guidelines for parenting. This inner wisdom is such an amazing fact that it is easy to discount or disbelieve. It is also a key to humanness and a valuable guide for parents.

Even though the wise feelings are there, it does not follow that the child knows what to do about them. It is the role of parents to learn to understand and read the needs of the child. A common signal of fatigue is being fussy. The child is tired, needs a nap or at least a rest, and she starts to fuss or fret. A command of 'stop fussing' misses the point, the direction of 'it is time for a story and a rest' is very much more to the point when the child is tired. If the child is thirsty or hungry, obviously rest time is not going to correct that. The Sage's guidance of "Know Thyself" is increased for parents to "Know Thyself and Know Thy Child".

When a child is sick, we may use a thermometer to take her temperature, and again we are reading nature's wisdom in response to an imbalance in the body. We trust thermometers to measure temperature, we trust barometers for measuring the pressure of the atmosphere. We need to learn to trust ourselves in reading feelings. Your feelings, my feelings, and your child's feelings measure inner comfort or discomfort, and the harmony or disharmony between the inner and outer worlds is another indicator of humanness.

The concept of a child as an unfolding unique individual with feelings to guide us in her care may be a new, perhaps even a strange idea. TV gives the message that the human body is a machine, sometimes dignified by being described as the 'most perfect' machine. Teachers sometimes copy this analogy. Is that possible? It seems possible in some jobs where employees are asked to perform like a machine: "Don't think or feel, just produce." We hear our heart referred to as a pump; we can now be given interchangeable parts – a transplanted heart, liver or kidney, plastic joints . . . Technology has found a way to treat the human body as a machine. That has been possible only since a medication has been developed that overrides the body's inner wisdom to reject foreign tissue. It is an interesting way of looking at scientific progress!

Machines can't grow

A machine is something that is made of physical material to perform a particular function. It is not born, but man-made. It does not breathe, feel or reproduce. If it is worn out at night, it is still worn out in the morning. It does not have the capacity to be rejuvenated by sleep. If it gets scraped or scratched, a machine does not have the ability to heal itself.

A machine does not grow or develop; the way it is made is the way it stays. A machine does not have hidden talents waiting to be nurtured and allowed to unfold. A machine is what man created it to be, no more. It is an idea of man that is made by man and is limited by the idea of the man who designed and built it. That is not a description of any child or adult. Man is not a machine nor should he be treated as one.

Animal instincts

There is also the concept that man is an animal and animals are used in research to understand problems of humans. How do humans differ from animals? Animals at birth are able to walk, to go to the mother for nourishment. Chicks peck their way out of the shell into the world and complete their own birth. Beavers build dams and some birds migrate. Animals have instincts developed far beyond those of man.

The size and appearance of a baby animal when it becomes

an adult of the species is fairly predictable. We see a baby lion and we know what it will look like as an adult lion. If we have studied the habits of a group of lions we can pretty well predict the habits of other lions: what food they will eat, when they will hunt, how the male and female will relate to each other and the cubs. Animals in their natural setting are predictable and have wise instincts.

Animals do not compose songs, paint pictures, make machines, create political parties, develop philosophies, build churches, have wars over different belief systems, or speak different languages in differents parts of the world. Humans do all these things and more. Animal sounds are determined by their species, and the sounds of each are recognizable and predictable. Their characteristic sounds appear to be instinctive and relatively unchanging.

Uniquely human qualities

Babies at an early age seek communication and learn the language of their parents through imitation. Language is learned by hearing others speak. Speech is not instinctive but learnt by listening and imitation.

At about one year of age the child strives to move in an upright position; then she has a very different view of the world. Standing up makes it easier to look down at the ground and up to the sky as well as straight ahead. Above and below become natural experiences. Just once in my lifetime have I seen a cow looking at the sky, and I experienced that as a remarkable event – driving by a meadow I saw just one cow looking upward at a kite that was floating overhead. All the other cows in the herd had their characteristic pose of head down grazing. Yet it is not at all amazing to see people looking at kites or birds or stars in the sky.

Another important difference between humans and animals are our hands, two hands and two feet. We do not need four feet for walking so we can have hands with fingers and a thumb. We can use our hands to write, draw, play musical instruments, do surgery, dentistry, sew, knit, carve, or make machines. To be human means to have the ability to stand upright, to speak a language, and to think about thoughts. From these capacities we have developed art, science, religion, history, philosophy, architecture, medicine . . . the list goes on. Animals, if given a fair chance by man, live their lives quite contentedly without needing to study any of these subjects.

Please note that these are not scored in competition to one another. There is no ranking that this is better and that is worse. There are differences, and we lose our sense of reality if we do not make the distinction. To parent a child we need to focus on *human* traits and allow them to develop, not try to create a human machine or an animal.

Chapter 3

Allowing Humanness

You are human and I am human. We stand upright on two feet, we speak and write words to connect with each other. When we do not speak a common language communication becomes much more difficult. We have our own ideas and we think about the ideas of others. That is all part of being human. Being human includes the capacity to be able to learn how to read and how to write. Today that is such a universal human ability that we generally give very little thought to it. We may be eager for our children to learn how to read and be pleased to tell our friends about precocious development, but we probably are not too amazed at having that ability. It is an ability that humans have and animals and machines do not have.

Human thinking

Not only are we able to read, we are also able to think about what we have read. We not only recognize the words, we also understand their meaning. Somehow we learn to put together new information with previous learning and we say "that makes sense" or "that does not make sense". In some mental illnesses that ability is lost. The way we increase our knowledge and learn about reality is by adding related thoughts to the concepts that we have. It is also important to reject unrelated thoughts. We have the capacity to sort out what is true from what is not true.

Although we have this capacity, the ability is not always developed. Whether we hear or read ideas it is important to think about what we have heard or read, and then to decide if it is true or not true. Just because something is written or has been spoken does not necessarily make it true. When we are given new information we have the task of deciding for ourselves if it is true. That does not mean we have to reject something if we are not sure about it. We have the additional option of taking it as a possibility if we are unsure if it fits with what we already know.

It is possible to develop a sense of truth, an inner experience that allows us to consider what we hear or read and then decide if it is true. This is a vital human ability to develop. Basic to developing a sense of truth is telling the truth. It is difficult to recognize realities, capacities or talents that you do not have yourself. If you are tone deaf it is not possible to tune a violin. So it is with truth. If you don't value truth and practise it, guard it, you won't be able to recognize it or the lack of it in the world.

We need to differentiate seeking and speaking the truth from trying to convince others that our thoughts are right and that they should agree with us. When we want others to agree with us and accept our ideas or prejudices we have strayed away from the important idea of freedom of thought. We need to seek what is true and allow others the opportunity to seek what is true. We can find agreement in seeking what is true, not in trying to direct or coerce others. Speaking clearly and thinking clearly are models we must present to our children.

Cleverness, deception, being a trickster have not always been admired traits. A devious person who did not tell the truth used to be thought of as unethical. Unfortunately our awareness of that has diminished. Dishonesty somehow has been accepted as almost inevitable; this is another twist that makes both parenting and learning as children more difficult today. Values have been lost or, perhaps worse, subverted.

Heartfelt thinking

When thoughts and ideas are used to deceive or trick people we find thinking without morality. If we use words to manipulate someone into doing what we want them to do we are thinking without connecting with our feelings. Promoting our own ideas to bring about what we want is a misuse of thinking.

When we use our thinking to find what is true and warm it with understanding we are using our human capacities in a healthy way. When we are concerned about the feelings of others we choose our words with care. Thinking clearly and speaking kindly are important goals for adults.

It is important to learn to think for ourselves. We each have our own feelings, our likes and dislikes, our own desires. When we allow the reality of individual thinking and individual feeling we gain a sound basis for parenting.

Recognizing feelings

Thoughts are expressed in words. Words give a reality to them that we can experience. All thoughts are not expressed, but enough of them are expressed for us to experience them. Feelings can be more elusive. Sometimes actions are a reflection of feelings and sometimes facial expressions are, but not always. Most of us learn to hide our feelings at least part of the time.

It is important to remember that feelings are neither right nor wrong. They just *are*. Learning to be aware of our own feelings is a useful skill to develop. Knowing our personal preferences is another human capacity, another aspect of our personal self. By being aware of our likes and dislikes we increase our own inner experiences of our personal self.

Children are born with feelings, and often we are able to accept the feelings of an infant to guide us in his care. It is his experience of his feelings that lets us know when he is cold, hungry, frightened or happy and contented. If we can accept and acknowledge the growing child's feelings and our own in the same way, it will help the child develop an acceptance of and awareness of his feelings as part of his humanness. That may seem self-evident but it is not always so easy. If at grandmother's house your child says, "I don't like this food", how will you respond to this spoken feeling? Will you be able to accept that feeling without being involved in a family episode? That will depend a lot on how your family looks at children expressing their own feelings, likes and dislikes. In many families it would be objected to.

Hopefully, such expression will be allowed while encouraging consideration of the feelings of others. The challenge is to recognize that the child is feeling upset or troubled, is having a problem and has not yet learned an appropriate way to convey that to others. More learning is needed and that is what childhood is for. You can not change or direct how he feels, we need to recognize that we each have our own feelings. We can help with his way of telling us how he feels.

A different kind of experience with expressing feelings is when your child says, "I am afraid to go to school" and in your effort to reassure him you respond with "No you are not, there is nothing for you to be afraid of". That is discounting the child's feelings, and this increases his problem. When your child expresses fear about a future event such as going to school, you need to acknowledge that feeling, then try to understand what is causing the feeling and reassure your child that you will help him deal with whatever is causing the concern. You first assure him that you are aware of his feelings and then that you will do what needs to be done to help him and protect him.

It is important that you follow through and do that. A child quickly learns whether or not he can count on his parents to be there for him. A reassurance without a follow up will seem like a deception to him and probably increase his anxiety. Recognizing that feelings are part of humanness may lead you into some learning times that most of us would prefer to avoid.

Handling negative feelings

An inevitable experience for children is having an activity stopped that they want to continue, or an activity started that they want to avoid. What needs to happen and what your child wants to happen will not always be the same thing. Children do not always appreciate our interventions, but the parent is the responsible one. When children are upset their words can hurt us. No parent likes to hear the words "I hate you" from their child, but chances are they have heard those words somewhere in their life experience and will call on them when they feel angry or frustrated.

Words can hurt and shock us, and that is important for us to remember in our own speech, and important for children to learn from us. If you have the unfortunate experience of being told, "I hate you", you try to remain calm, to acknowledge that he is upset, feeling frustrated, not liking your decision, but you carry through with whatever needs to be done. At a later time you can tell him that it hurts your feelings when he says that and it is not alright. Going through life telling people that you hate them does not enhance social relationships and part of your parenting goal is to help your child function in the world in a successful way.

Talking about it later, rather than when the explosion occurs, gives the child a better chance of being able to take in what you have to say. In the heat of anger it is difficult to be aware of the other person's needs and feelings. It will help to give him other words that he can use the next time he feels that way. Perhaps find ways to say what it is that he want to do. It might be, "I'm not finished yet", or "I want to keep playing". Finding words for what he wants to do is preferable to telling how he feels about others. Our goal is to acknowledge our own feelings and the feelings of others, while using words in a considerate way. Verbal explosions do not enhance humanness. Helping your child express himself verbally does not mean that you will agree to let him continue playing when it is time to stop. When we acknowledge each other's feelings, we are relating with understanding and that can diffuse many disagreements.

Allowing individuality

Another important capacity for mature adults, and one that needs to be high on our list of future goals for our child, is developing an awareness of his own unique self, knowing his self and valuing it. Unless or until we know ourselves as unique individuals we will not recognize that reality in others. It must be thought about because in our daily life the world does not often have an awareness of the dignity of the individual and of the value of individuality.

We each have our own feelings based on our particular sensitivities, our own life experiences, our individual temperaments. We have our own thoughts that are a sum total of what we have learned in our lives. Each of us has had different life experiences so we each have a different data base of thoughts that we have learned from life. The richer our life's experience has been, the more aware we have been of what is going on around us, the more talents that we have unfolded, the more attention we have given to our own feelings, the more we think for ourselves, the better chance we will have of deciding what we as individuals value and believe. An important human goal for each of us is to learn to think for ourselves and also to be aware of our own feelings.

These are goals for adult human beings, not an expectation we have of a child. By being aware of our ideal for a healthy adult human being, we strive for those qualities in ourselves, allow the child to experience the qualities in us, but we do not expect them in our children. Rather we will provide our children with the varied life experiences necessary to be able to develop those qualities.

How you respond to "I don't like that" at mealtimes will involve more than what is said at the moment. What is your attitude toward eating what has been served? Do you know that his feelings can include food likes and dislikes? Do both parents agree? It is amazing what a loaded situation mealtimes can be and we will discuss that at length later. For now we are looking at the expression of feelings and your acknowledgement of their expression. First you need to let him know that you are aware that he is having a problem with what has been served.

The problem increases when you are concerned with more than one person's feelings, thoughts, and reactions. When you are more concerned about not causing problems than you are in dealing realistically with the situation, your decision becomes even more difficult. Whatever you do will be a learning experience for the child. When you regard each person's feelings, whether of an adult or a child, you go a long way toward bridging the differences. When you let the other person know that you accept his feelings, then he is affirmed and allowed to be who he is. That is a basic need for all of us. When your personal self acknowledges the other's personal self communication is enhanced.

Although we want to acknowledge the feelings of the child it is also important for the child to learn that others have feelings too. At times it is appropriate to let the child know how he is making others feel and at other times that will unnecessarily confuse and escalate the problem. "How To" books can not tell you what to do in each situation, only out of your own understanding and awareness can you choose what is best to do in a specific situation.

Being human involves having needs, feelings and thoughts and acting on them. If we remind ourselves that each of us has our own separate thoughts and feelings and include that in our effort to understand each other, relationships will become easier to manage. If you try to figure out on your own what someone else thinks or tell them how they should feel, life will be a frustrating and unrewarding journey for both of you. It is wonderful to experience thoughts in common and have feelings in common with others, but only when they are personally real is it a real human experience.

When we maintain our personal self while allowing the feelings and needs of the child to speak to us, we are meeting the inner developing being of the child. We are allowing a space for his reality to live in the world and that provides the child with the opportunity to trust in himself and to be an individual. Young children learn from imitation and when the parents relate to each other with respect for the feelings and thoughts of each other, the child has a head start in learning what it means to be a healthy human. Children learn more from what is done in their presence than they do from threats, admonitions, or demands that they behave in a certain way.

As with eating and breathing, the child takes in what is in the outer world and makes that part of himself. What is in the outer world becomes part of the child's inner world. Nurturing and nourishing can become part of the child's personality if he has had the opportunity of experiencing that in his world. Allowing the child to discover his own ideas, experience his own feelings and be aware of the feelings of others provides that nurturing experience for him.

By growing up in a healthy environment that values humanness and allows individuality to unfold, he will know from his own first hand experience what a responsible free individual is. Then he won't need to spend his time reading books about personal development and parenting skills.

Chapter 4

The Child meets the World

One of life's challenges is balancing the needs of individuals with the needs of society. In family life it is balancing harmony among family members with individual needs. What is wanted by one person may not be in the best interest of the group. Finding the optimal balance and helping children learn this consideration of others takes heartfelt thinking. Teaching the necessary skills for a child to live in harmony in social groups while maintaining her individuality is an important parenting task.

A traditional way of teaching family rules is through compliance and obedience. How does that relate to our parenting goals? When do we want children to obey and comply with our demands and expectations? Certainly when a danger is present we need to act in a decisive way and expect the child to follow directions. We want that, but we eventually want the child to be able to develop an inner awareness, her own sense of what is right to do and what is dangerous or unacceptable. Our parenting goal is to have adults who can think for themselves, be responsible for themselves, make their own healthy choices, have their own expectations.

The parent's role will vary greatly depending on the age of the child. A toddler will be totally without inner resources to direct her own exploring of the world and we need to be very attentive to what she is doing. During toddler time the responsibility is all ours and we want to make certain that we are always providing a safe environment for exploring the world.

Learning boundaries

Getting angry at a toddler for exploring helps no one. Exploration is in the nature of a healthy toddler. Activity is a natural process that allows the child to learn to crawl and walk and explore the world. Learning what is acceptable to explore and how to explore are necessary for social learning. Helping the child learn to direct her activity in a safe and acceptable way is the parent/teacher task. Parents need to help children learn what to do as well as what not to do. If parents are consistent, the toddler will learn the boundaries and live with them.

When parents respond to unacceptable exploring with suggestions or directions for acceptable exploring the child learns what *to do*. If you are busy in the kitchen and your little one opens the drawer of place mats and linens, tell her: "that drawer needs to be closed, find your drawer". Obviously, this presumes forethought on your part that you have set aside a drawer with interesting kitchen items that are safe to explore. Her drawer could have an assortment of unbreakable, expendable items gleaned from your own kitchen or smaller toy kitchen items. Perhaps you suggest that she set up a party for her doll or let her "wash" her bowls in the sink. She will want to do what she has seen you doing. Children learn through play. When they play they imitate the adult world and practise for it. Playing is their way of learning, practising for life.

Humans have three basic ways of learning: imitation, direction, and discovery. For children social rules are best learned through imitation of you as a good role model, and by your telling them what *to do* (direction). If you yell, criticize, or punish, then the child learns from discovery what *not to do* but that leaves what *to do* a blank slate.

When the child is doing something that the parent thinks of as wrong, the first question needs to be; "Has she learned how to do it right?" Sometimes the answer will be "yes" and sometimes "no". Learning takes practice. Remind the child of your expectations, help her learn and when necessary interrupt the behaviour that you do not approve of. First give a verbal reminder and if necessary a physical intervention. If the toddler reaches for something that will burn her, say "no, hot", while physically interrupting her reaching to prevent her from getting burned. Then she will learn that your "no" is protective, that she can count on you to help her and guide her in this complicated world. If instead you get angry and yell, or hit her, she will feel vulnerable and fearful. Depending on the child's temperament a child who feels threatened will be likely to either respond to power with her own attempt at power, or take on the role of a victim. Neither are desirable responses. The world does not need tyrants or victims. We need responsible people.

If the little one is repeatedly turning the radio switch on and off you say "that is not to play with" or "that hurts the radio". If she is turning it on and it is not the appropriate time you say, "it is not time for the radio now, I will tell you when you can turn it on". Help her learn. Help her know what to do and when to do it. As new experiences occur, new learning will have to take place.

Save "no" for the most important issues. A child who hears "no" too often soon learns to ignore it. "No" fails to have a special meaning.

Guiding interests

Toddlers are easily redirected to other activities and that is the approach to use with them most of the time. Exploration of the world is a natural event for a toddler, and we want to allow and keep alive this natural expression of interest in the world. It is interest in the world that motivates us to learn about how things work, what things do and what is happening in the world around us. The nature of a child compels her to be doing things.

A young child's first exploration of books is at risk for being book destruction time without parental guidance. If children see you being careful with books they may learn that through imitation. But they will probably need you to direct them to carefully hold the book on their lap, carefully turn the pages from the corner one at a time, and when they are finished with it, help them put it back in its place. It helps if you say "this is the book's place or the book's home". The child then has an introduction into the world of books. She learns to care for them and value them. She cannot know how to handle books without help.

When a child's interest in exploring her world is discouraged, apathy develops and that interferes with learning and social responsibility. Being a healthy child and being passive are mutually exclusive. Children need direction in learning appropriate ways to use their activity, to explore and learn about the world. Remember we are thinking of tomorrow as well as today. Although redirecting is our primary method for toddlers, there are times when "no" is needed. Some behaviour is never allowed.

The rule of three

A good guide for knowing when to use "no" is the Rule of Three: it is never all right to intentionally hurt yourself, hurt others, or destroy property. Those three acts are always "no". We never laugh, or give any indication of approval that any of those three events are ever tolerated or accepted. By saving our "no" for those three behaviours we focus the child's attention on our disapproval of destructive and aggressive behaviour.

Until we tell them, children have no way of knowing that it hurts the cat when they step on his tail or squeeze him too hard. Neither can we expect them to discriminate between real and stuffed animals. It is desirable that they should be careful with their stuffed toys too, but essential that they learn kindness to real animals. If we yell "you are a bad girl" she will believe that, but she still will not have learned how to pet a cat. Children believe what their parents say and they will believe that they are bad, but they won't have learned how to play with a cat in a kind way. One of our tasks is to help them learn about the world and learn appropriate ways to live in the world and to care about others. We need to show them how to pet the cat gently, how to be careful. We need to tell them what to do more often than we tell them what not to do. Then they learn not only about the cat but also about us and our role in their lives. If we only say "don't hurt the cat" and the cat is still there, they have not learned what to do and their natural interest will lead them to continue exploring the cat.

Their natural enthusiasm may always get the better of them; so you not only need to teach them what to do, but you also need to monitor them to assure that they are practising what you want them to learn. They have to learn how to behave and we need to be their teachers. Remember that teaching is what you do; learning is what they do. Just because you have taught something once does not mean that they have learned it forever.

Toddlers are not one trial learners, they learn from repeated consistent responses. Don't think if you have told them something once then they "should" know what to do. Understanding the word "should" is remarkably valuable for parents. Every time I have heard a person say "he should" or "she should" or "you should" they have really meant "I want". "He should know by now" translates to "I

want him to know by now"; "he should be able to" translates to "I
want him to be able to". Be aware any time you hear yourself saying
"should" that you probably are not giving clear messages and it may
lead to conflict or misunderstanding. When someone says to you,
"you should" you can silently rephrase it to its real meaning of "they
want me to", and save yourself a frustrating interaction.

The Rule of Three is a good guide throughout life. It does not
matter what the age of the person, it still applies. It is never all right
to intentionally hurt yourself, hurt others, or damage property.
When children experience this at an early age and later hear it said,
then an important value system is in place. They will have a basis for
their own choices and judgments later on. As they get older and are
faced with making their own choices they will have some concepts to
guide them. Following the Rule of Three for a lifetime is not the
same as remaining obedient and compliant. Rather it is using values
that have been learned and lived by, and applying them to new
situations.

Learning from the environment

In an ideal world, a child would live in an environment that
manifests healthy living, consideration of others, healthy ethics,
morality and virtue. Then through imitating her environment she
would learn socially appropriate behaviour. What a child
instinctively imitates as a toddler and young child soon becomes a
habit and then becomes a personal trait. An obvious example of this
is speech. Children imitate the speech of their parents and learn the
mother tongue. The child hears the sounds, imitates them and the
parents' language becomes the child's language. A child who hears
little speech will learn less speech. Children also learn forbidden
words if they hear them spoken. If they live with people who are
considerate, polite, respect each other and say "thank you" and
"please", that will become a habit with them, too. They will not have
to be told what to say, they will have learned from imitation.
Children take in what is in their environment and it becomes a part
of them. What is in the outer world becomes part of their inner
world. Familiar words and familiar interactions that are imitated and
encouraged become part of the child's personality.

Very early in a child's life she is learning from imitation. Early examples of behaviour learned through imitation are waving bye-bye and playing patty-cake. The child sees the parent do it and imitates what she sees in the world. That is the primary learning process in the young child. If the parent and toddler together wash their hands before meals, brush their teeth before bedtime, use the toilet at regular times, they become habits for the child and are easily encouraged.

Children need to learn about taking care of themselves. They do not automatically know when to brush their teeth, wash their hands and use the toilet. We need to teach them about those things out of our own understanding. We need to teach how, but also we need to teach when. Regular toileting habits can prevent unpleasant accidents, discomfort and power struggles. Good habits let us care for ourselves in an orderly way. Learning to use the toilet when she first wakes up, washing her hands after toiletting, and brushing her teeth after she has washed her hands are important morning sequences to learn. Using the toilet before meals and washing hands before meals go together in a natural way. Toiletting before going on an outing as well as before bedtime are great habits to start at an early age.

There are convenient regular times for personal care and grooming, and the child who learns that early will be spared inconvenient interruptions. The occasional "I do not need to now" can be answered with a pleasant "just try". A young child by nature wants to be like the adults in her life and you want to use these early years wisely and establish rhythms and habits that will help the child in later years. When the child has learned about life by doing it with you and later can do it on her own, it is a pleasant experience for both the parents and the child. It is the most natural way of learning how to do things which can later be done on her own, a healthy way of becoming a separate responsible, self dependent individual.

Valuing harmony

It is in young children's nature to want to please their parents in order to be in harmony with them. Their natural interest leads them to explore and experiment with the world and the people in it but ultimately healthy people value and thrive on harmony; children want to please others. Adults, too, want to please people whom they care about. Humans are social beings and peace is more rewarding than war or conflict. If harmony was in your environment as you were growing up, you have an inner sense of that.

The child who learns healthy human behaviour from the parents as role models learns the value of warmth and caring, and experiences human harmony and the dignity of man. Then out of her own life experience she will learn about being understanding and reasonable. She will have her inner dignity validated and know that she, too, is of value to the world.

When we demand compliance we are deciding what another person's actions are to be. Taking on that responsibility is appropriate with the very young child and in fact she will look to us for that. As the child grows and learns, we need to be willing to allow the child to use what she has learned, encourage her to think for herself, to direct her own actions when she is able. It is part of giving over to the child what she is able to do when she is able. When we continue to decide what is right for another individual to do, we are disallowing her own talents, inner thoughts, feelings, needs and self. The inner reality, the inner wisdom is part of our own humanness and needs to be recognized and allowed to develop.

Our goal is for the child eventually to learn to make her own right choices. First the parent makes the choices out of what is right for the child so that the child can later make her own choices out of what is right for her. When a child has learned to make healthy choices and act on them she will feel good about herself. A child who feels good about herself does not get into trouble, does not hurt others, does not destroy property or treat others with contempt. If the parent has made decisions out of the needs of the child; recognizing her individuality, knowing her feelings, listening to her thoughts, helping her experience being in harmony with the environment, then she will have the basis for finding a healthy way into the world. The parent will have helped the child learn the value of being considerate towards others as well as being aware of and considering herself.

The child who sees and experiences parents considering each other's needs, the child's needs, the brothers' and sisters' needs, will learn about healthy family life and social living. A group of people who care about each other, neither disregarding themselves nor each other, learn that fairness does not mean that everyone has the same thing. It means acknowledging each other's individual needs, feelings, and thoughts, and treating each other with consideration. A healthy balance between awareness of ourself and awareness of others allows us to live in harmony with others. Being a balanced person and being in harmony with others are qualities we want to help our children develop. Balance and harmony are human values that can be learned and need to be practised to become life-long inner traits. When we live out of higher ideals, beyond instincts, with a sense of responsibility and caring, then we celebrate our humanness.

Chapter 5

Punishment or Discipline

As well as the parent, the teacher is also the role model from whom the child learns, and it is important to be aware of what methods are being used. Is harmony sought through punishment or discipline? One question is often whether to spank or not to spank. The words discipline and punishment are often used interchangeably, leading us to think of them as synonyms, and that can make learning about parenting more difficult. Words do have real meanings, represent reality, but in our world of illusion and confusion it is not always easy to sort through to the real meaning of words.

It is not uncommon today to have someone discount differences by saying that it is only a matter of semantics. The implication is that both people mean the same thing, they are just using different words. That probably is not the case. The reality is that we need to use the word that gives the exact meaning of what we are thinking to be able to communicate clearly. We also need to recognize the importance of subtle but often immensely significant differences.

Understanding the difference

Discipline relates to disciple, the one who leads others. Punishment, derived from puneo, means to punish, to inflict pain on others. A leader of others is experienced very differently from one who inflicts pain on others. It is the difference between helping and hurting.

Being aware that children imitate what they see, what is in their environment, it becomes clear that discipline and punishment will have very different effects on children. The parent who says, "I'll teach you to hit your brother", and then slaps the child, will be doing just what she has said. She is teaching that the bigger person can inflict pain on the smaller person.

Take time to think about your own parenting style and decide which you use more often. Being aware of the difference and the different effects on your child will help you grow as a parent. Both discipline and punishment involve an interaction between one person who knows what is acceptable and appropriate and one who apparently does not know. They both give the impression of a relationship where one is in charge, and the other is a learner. Punishment relies on the stronger person using power to control the weaker one. Discipline relies on knowledge that one is wiser, a teacher, and the other a learner. Discipline depends on respect, punishment on submission.

Punishment by definition means to inflict pain, restrain, or penalize for a fault or an offence. It is hard to think of it as a kind or loving experience. It is an action taken to show that we do not like what has been done, it refers to a past event. It shows disapproval and is intended to cause discomfort or suffering. Hitting, slapping, spanking, and restricting are punishments commonly used by parents. Punishment gives a penalty for something already done. Punishment does not teach what is right, it teaches what happens when we or someone else does something wrong. Its message is 'do not do that again'. Punishment gives a penalty for something already done. Punishment does not teach what is right, it teaches what happens when we or someone else does something wrong. Its message is 'do not do that again'. Punishment is also used as a deterrent to make others aware of possible unpleasant future consequences. The more sensitive child learns from, and may be frightened by, the punishment of another child.

Punishment works with power. If we look at our own experiences it is clear that we are not intimidated by people unless they have some power or control over us. Without some basis of control, intimidation may make us feel uncomfortable, but it is not likely to change our behaviour. Threats of punishment without the power to control are likely to bring on the thought 'you can't make me'. One thing that is learned from punishment is that stronger people can hurt weaker people and they can use that strength as power to control. That is a reality of life. Another reality is that most of us resent or fear the person who uses their power to control us. We admire the person who uses their power to help those who are vulnerable, less powerful.

Power needs

It is true that some behaviour can be controlled by punishment or threat of punishment, as long as the punisher has the power to control the other person. Punishment or fear of punishment is less likely to control behaviour when the person is away from the controller. It is not the basis of developing conscience. Quite the opposite, when away from the power it will be tempting to misbehave to prove to yourself that there are limits to the other person's power. For punishment to work, power or threat of power has to be maintained and that is difficult to do for 18 years. It is quite possible that at some point the child will become stronger than the parent and then that kind of parent power is gone.

The power symbols for adults may be the police or the boss at work, or the family member with some means of control who forces us into compliance. If you are able to get in touch with your feelings in those situations you will discover they are not pleasant, warm feelings. In fact they lead to feelings of being powerless, helpless or dependent, and the temptation is to do what you need to do to get over those feelings, to find a way to regain some power of your own.

When parents make children please them out of fear of parent power, that is not the basis for healthy human development. The child that fears a parent will not have a relationship built on mutual trust, respect, and concern. Obedience and compliance do not lead to self discipline and self control. They lead to behaving to please others to avoid the negative consequences. When we are intimidated we acknowledge that someone has power over us, is stronger than we are, and can make our life unpleasant and uncomfortable. We have to do what they want. It is not possible to have warm, loving feelings for someone whose power and control we have to submit to. You may align yourself with that power to protect yourself, even grab some power for yourself, but that is not the same as caring about the person.

Learning respect

Discipline does not involve power, it relates to respect. Discipline is successful because it fits with a young child's natural tendency to look up to a stronger, wiser person, an authority. It is successful between people who care about each other. Most of us want to please people we like, admire, care about. That is a different experience from feeling we have to please people because we are afraid of them. When, out of our inner freedom, we try to please people that we care about, we experience the harmony that comes from cooperation. Learning to cooperate, to consider others, is a skill we want to teach children so that they can be at ease while playing or working with others.

Appropriate discipline will provide children with a chance to learn about consequences in the world, a valuable thing to know about. Being aware of what punishment is and of how that makes the punisher and the punished feel, is important in parenting as well as awareness of discipline and cooperation. When we are not clear about these differences our parenting task is more difficult.

When a parent only focuses on obedience, compliance, power, and control, they risk missing the humanness of the child and instead are responding to the child as a machine or an animal. We do need to *control* machines, we *train* animals, but we want to *teach* children. At first it is difficult to distinguish between these approaches but it is essential if we are going to sort out our tasks as parents, our purpose and the consequences of what we are doing.   Parenting needs to be a conscious art. As a society we need to discover what has been missing in the lives of children who are in trouble, who have grown up to be troubled adults, and cause trouble for themselves and for society.

Social consciousness

The passive person who has given up his own inner sense of himself lacks the ability to make his own individual choices. He is at risk of becoming victim to a cult leader, or to peer group pressures that can manipulate his behaviour. An inner sense of good and bad, right and wrong is a necessity in today's world of confused social values. You will be a follower, a puppet, a robot without this inner self, and that is not healthy humanness. Machines need controls to direct their power, they don't have an inner reality of feelings, thoughts or values. Animals are not expected to make ethical choices or to have a social consciousness and we train them to meet our social expectations.

Man's ability to control animals risks giving him an unhealthy sense of power and control that holds a fascination for some. The epitome of this is perhaps the lion tamer, but we see it with family pets and other animals, too. It is worthwhile wondering about the value of animal obedience training when it is extended beyond socializing the animal. It is important to think about how it fits into our goals of being healthy human beings. We need to be very careful about how we use power. We also need to differentiate between training animals and teaching children.

The parent has the task of helping the child learn what is expected in our world and also helping the child develop an inner sense of self as the first step to self control. The self is an essential part of self control. Learning only to surrender to power and control through obedience and compliance stifles the qualities needed to become a responsible adult. It is important to know what we are really doing in our relationship with children if we are going to be successful. Parenting will involve some punishment and some discipline.

Behaviour is learned

When we realize that discipline is what teaches consequences and helps the child learn the value of appropriate behaviour we can value its place in the life of the child. When faced with misbehaviour we need to remember to ask ourselves, "Has the child learned the right way to behave and is he capable of doing it on his own?" Learning takes practice and it is important to be aware of that, too.

When punishment seems called for it is important that it fits the misdeed. When punishment is extreme or too severe the child is more likely to resent the punishment than learn the lesson that was intended.

Important goals in parenting are: helping our children be successful; helping them learn appropriate behaviour; helping them learn about natural consequences in the world, and preparing them to be able to make their own choices. Remembering that behaviour is learned, we must not expect our children to know until they have had the chance to learn. When confronted with behaviour that we do not approve of we ask ourselves where and how did the child learn that behaviour. Knowing that behaviour is learned we realize that new, more appropriate, behaviour can be learned to replace what we do not approve of. Children are learning all the time and parents and teachers are teaching all the time, sometimes from direction and sometimes through examples. It is very important to remember that a child imitates in order to learn. Of course, children also learn from other children, other adults, movies, television and whatever they see and hear.

Nothing is gained by feeling guilty about the inappropriate behaviour of your child; there is much to be gained by realizing that you can help him learn what you feel is important and valuable. Respecting your child so that he can learn to respect others is essential in parent-child learning. Being the role model, helping your child learn by giving him consistent rules and natural consequences are all a part of discipline. The wiser you are, the more able you are to teach acceptable behaviour, the less you will need to resort to punishment.

Chapter 6

From Discipline to Self-discipline

The ultimate goal of discipline is self discipline, the ability to be responsible for oneself and to have respect for others. In order that the child can reach the goal of self discipline we need to provide the rules of discipline and the model of self control while also helping the child develop a sense of self. Self discipline requires both learning discipline and being aware of self. We want the child eventually to learn to cooperate with rules out of an inner directedness, an inner desire to act in a responsible way. The obedient child has been asked to give the control of her actions to others, to be submissive, and is not developing a healthy sense of self or any ability to think for herself. She is learning submission to others rather than learning to be aware of and respect others.

Learning healthy choices

To be a responsible, cooperative adult requires thinking for yourself and making healthy choices for yourself while having consideration for others. To be able to function well as an informed, thinking, compassionate citizen in a free world requires being able to make informed healthy choices based on an ethical awareness of your self, of others, and of the world. Self control and self discipline are our final goals and childhood is the time the child has to learn about and develop these abilities. The parent must make decisions based on the needs of the child while considering the needs of others. In parenting we need to recognize that the child too has individual needs. Recognizing the child's individual needs, feelings and thoughts affirms the individuality of the child and allows the child the opportunity of developing her sense of self. The parent has the task of teaching appropriate behaviour, stopping destructive behaviour, building the child's sense of self without allowing tyranny. This becomes a real balancing act and balance is a key to a healthy personality. Healthy humanness is a balance: neither self-seeking while disregarding others nor pleasing others while disregarding self. A harmony of I and Thou. Balance and harmony are keys to healthy social interaction and they have to be learned in stages.

Finding balance

Balance and harmony are recurring themes in the natural and the man made world. We value balance especially in art and harmony in music. The child has an instinctive relationship to balance in his early years which we can observe in his physical development. Balance is learned slowly and in stages. Walking unassisted is the culmination of one year's experience with balance. A child learns to walk by balancing right-left, front-back, up-down. Too far in any direction and down she goes. It is a skill that typically takes about twelve months to achieve.

There are many steps required before getting to balance in walking. First the baby has to learn to balance her head and develop head control. That has to be accomplished before the baby can develop trunk control. Learning to balance on her own while sitting is another significant development and this same trunk control then enables the child to scoot and crawl. Last comes the limb control which allows the child to balance standing upright and completes the development necessary before she can learn to walk unassisted. The many steps needed are achieved from the head down.

To be able to walk the child has to be able to balance well enough to be able to lean forward slightly to be able to move ahead. The child tries and falls, then tries again and falls again, but she does not give up. Her parents encourage her, accept her attempts and do not criticize her for failed attempts.

Accepting a child's physical development is usually much easier for parents than accepting her social learning development. Some parents may try to speed up this physical process, may put the child in a "walker", but nature will be the final determiner of when it is time for the child to walk alone. The child's inner wisdom directs this development if the child is healthy. No matter what the parent prefers, the child's own nature determines when she is ready to walk.

Incidentally, putting a child in a "walker", giving an upright position before the earlier physical development is complete, can take away from the important stage of crawling. Studies on reading problems reveal the importance of the neurological development that occurs through crawling, part of nature's wisdom. Allowing the wisdom in nature to unfold in a natural way is a good guide to healthy child development. Trying to speed up the child's development may be an ego need of the parent, but it is not in the best interest of the child. We cannot expect the child to run or jump before she can walk, even if we want her to. A regular question in parenting needs to be, "Is it what I want or what is right for her?" This refers to a healthy child; when a child's natural development is delayed it is of great value to have therapeutic intervention. When the inner wisdom of the child is not unfolding, professional help is essential at an early age to enhance the child's development.

The stages of physical development may be easier to allow to develop because we can see them occurring in an orderly way which makes recognizing them and understanding them easier. The child's inner wisdom directs the physical development and the parents keep the environment safe to allow the development. In social learning the parent has the task of directing the social development out of their own learning and wisdom. This part of child development is our task. Social learning too needs to occur in stages and we need to be in tune with the natural sequence of learning in social skills and social behaviour.

Social learning

Learning social skills requires practice, just as learning physical skills. Both have to be practised to be able to develop. Appropriate behaviour must first be learned, then practised to become a personal trait. Appropriate behaviour is a balance – of personal inner needs, wants, and awareness of outer dangers and expectations, while considering other people's needs, ideas and customs. It is another balance to be discovered, practised and learned. This is a very important fact for parents to be aware of. Children do not learn in one attempt, they need several tries and they need consistent expectations and responses throughout these attempts. Parenting is most successful when parents are aware of the time needed for learning and the stages of development in the learning sequences. They also need to value consistency in their expectations.

Knowing that it takes about one year to learn to walk, and more years to run, skip, jump, skate and balance on a two-wheeler we can get a perspective on how long emotional balance and learning social behaviour can take. A child has to learn how to behave to maintain harmony with the others in his environment while also meeting his own needs in this complex world. Encouragement and success bring progress, good feelings, and the courage to keep trying. Nature gives humans an extended period for childhood, we need to recognize that and use it carefully. Learning to be appropriately assertive, but not too demanding, appropriately patient without being too passive, can be a lifelong learning task. When we are aware of the child's feelings and thoughts and help her to be aware of our feelings and thoughts we help her with this life's task.

Awareness of balance and harmony is necessary to bring about the desirable inner and outer harmony of the child with others in the family, later in the school, the neighbourhood, and the world. To teach healthy behaviour involves an awareness of individual needs, family needs, and social needs. The more we understand the developmental sequences in personality development, the easier it is to provide for the child's needs and learning opportunities at each stage.

To label developments as "just a stage" and avoiding teaching what the child easily learns at the time misses a good opportunity. Our goal is a healthy personality who has an inner balance and harmony and is in harmony with others, owning her own thoughts, feelings, and space, while allowing others their own feelings, thoughts, and space. Self control and self discipline are our final goals, but in the beginning of a child's life we need to start by recognizing that the child has an inner self with individual needs. We need to allow the developing sense of self, using our real self to relate to the reality of the child's separate self. We then give the child the experience of the meeting of two people who care about, consider and respect each other. I hope it is obvious that we don't tell the child this but allow the child the experience.

Personal values

The more we are able to model these traits, the better chance the child has of developing them. We always teach out of who we are. When we pursue an inner search for what is true, a desire for goodness, and a love of beauty we have the ideal combination that leads to healthy cooperative social interactions. Remembering that what the child experiences in his environment becomes her memory pictures, and what is imitated and experienced becomes a habit, we realize the importance of good examples in daily living.

Your own personal values will determine your responses to behaviour and what you want to teach your child; so it is important that you think about what is important to you and why. The parents who help the child learn what is appropriate social behaviour and who help the child do it out of his own sense of self provide a valuable basis for healthy human development. When we believe we are the only person with the right answer or the right way to do things then chances are we will be ignoring the individuality of others and telling them what to do. When we realize that everyone has the capacity to feel and later to learn to think and make their own choices we will accept those capacities in the child and help her develop her own inner resources.

When the child is misbehaving it is time to ask ourselves some questions. We need to ask what is going wrong, what is the child feeling or thinking. Am I expecting more than she can do? Does she need more direction or supervision? Does she need to learn a new behaviour or have more practice of a behaviour she is learning? If we jump to the judgment that 'she is bad', we skip the steps of understanding the situation and the chance to learn from it.

Sharing with others

If a four year old is grabbing a toy from her younger brother or sister, we need to step in, sort out ownership and direct appropriate ways to ask for the toy. Yelling 'bad girl' and slapping the grabber will not teach better behaviour for the future. Allowing the behaviour to continue without intervention will risk the behaviour becoming a habit. The older child will have difficulty learning the process of sharing with a new brother or sister unless we are there to help. Teaching sharing can be confusing for parents as they attempt to sort out what they believe is right.

Sharing is generally seen as a 'good' trait and 'good' children share. Wanting to teach their children what 'good children' do prompts parents to expect their children to share. Often parents think she 'should' want to share with her younger brother or sister or they may decide she *has* to share. If up until now all the toys in the house were hers this may be a difficult time for all concerned. Parents may tell the child that it is not nice not to share. We would guess what the child experiences then. If she could put her feelings in words, chances are she would say, 'he gets all the attention that I used to get and now I have to give him all my treasures too'. The young child will not have those concepts but most likely will have that experience. If your partner brought a new spouse into the family would you want to share?

Sharing means letting someone else use what I own. So first I have to know that I own it before I can share it. It is not possible to understand sharing before you understand ownership. If you own it, it means that it is yours. It does not mean that you have to give it to some one else. You also would have trouble understanding stealing if you did not understand ownership. If anyone can take anything of yours, it seems reasonable to expect that you can take anything of theirs. It is also important to remember that ownership is a man made construct, not something that is an ultimate truth. It is part of social learning, a learned concept. The concept of ownership leads us to value sharing and reject the unpleasant possibility of stealing. In our culture it is important to help children develop a sense of personal space and personal belongings, to learn about ownership so that they can respect others' space and personal belongings. We need to understand the meaning of what we are teaching, not just label behaviour as good or bad.

The first step for the child is learning about ownership and respecting others' ownership. You cannnot make someone share, sharing is an inner deed. You can make someone give up ownership, but that is not learning to share. When forced or demanded it is not sharing. Demands do not bring about an inner feeling of generosity. By acknowledging the feelings of the owner who has been asked to share and helping the child understand the needs and feeling of the other child, you provide a good basis for helping the child learn to share.

You can verbalize that the other child would like a turn, does not have anything to play with or do, whatever the reality is. Then the owner has a chance to think about the other person. If the child is still not ready to share, then help her offer some other toy or other solution to maintain the relationship. Perhaps the toy she is unable to share needs to be put away and another activity started. It is helpful to discuss the need to share before visitors come and prevent the problem by preparing ahead of time for the visit. Discuss with the child what is planned, and help her sort out what she is able to share and put away what she is not able to share. Then the child's conflict is acknowledged, and she has some time to think about how to handle it.

Sharing is a complicated event with many implications. When you see it as a difficult thing to learn and don't expect it to just happen, the child will probably learn it more easily. Learning the consequences of not sharing by having to play alone, or not being able to play with other children's toys, is something that should be pointed out, not used as a threat but stated as a reality. Generosity and sharing are real only when they are an inner feeling, when the inner self can let go and become aware of others' desires or needs.

Harmony with friends and family makes life meaningful and joyous. Being aware of each child's feelings and thoughts and helping them discover how others feel is a good basis for healthy friendships and relationships. It is a way to learn to respect others and to be responsible.

As parents our goal must be to rear a child to become an adult who has self control, self esteem, and self discipline. We want her to respect others and be responsible for herself. For her to achieve that goal we need to provide a model and give her opportunities to develop an awareness of herself and others. We must all find ways to meet our needs that are not at the expense of the needs of others, ways of relating to others with consideration and cooperation.

Chapter 7

Learning Values

As a child grows, imitates and feels involved with family life, he will have grown in ability and responsibility and want to help with family tasks and family activities. He will have an inner desire to do more grown-up things. One example could be his filling the glasses with milk. While pouring the milk, he accidentally knocks a glass over, breaks it and spills the milk, even though he was trying to be careful. How should a parent respond?

A punishment might be meted out, such as hitting him, or not allowing him to watch his favourite TV show, or being sent to his room. None of these responses will help him learn how to handle spills and broken glasses. The reality is, when anything is spilled, it has to be cleaned up, preferably by the person who has spilled it. When something is broken, it needs to be replaced. Discipline would involve having him help clean up the milk and pick up the broken glass. Depending on age and circumstances (if there are repeated accidents) it could also involve finding a way for him to pay for the broken glass. Discipline is a natural consequence that allows the child to learn what happens in the world.

Taking responsibility

Learning how to clean up spills thoroughly is an important thing to learn in the world. This, too, is best learned from imitation and direction. When you show your child what cleaning equipment to use and demonstrate how to use it, helping him learn, then he will eventually be able to clean up on his own. He will be able to take responsibility for the incident.

If the child is punished, then someone else will have to do the cleaning up and it will probably be you, and the next time and the time after that. A child that cleans up his own spills is not likely to spill on purpose and he does learn to be more careful. There are still consequences to spilling even if it is an accident. The spill still needs to be cleaned up and the glass replaced. If the deed is not being punished, but the consequences are being met, you won't be diverted by the "accident" theory and the clean up can proceed.

Spilling on purpose is unlikely, but there is a caveat. Remembering that part of 'learning is practice', the young child might enjoy the learning and 'accidentally' spill on purpose. That is when you put the child's feelings in words for him: "Do you like cleaning spills? Let's go to the sink and you can practise there."

Discipline directed by the parents and learned and practised by the child is the basis of self discipline in later years. It is learning about the real world and how to function successfully in it. Self discipline is a valuable trait in adult life and one that can be nurtured. Knowing how to clean up spills is also an important thing to learn. When you give up the role of boss and replace it with caring leader or director you have the basis for helping the child learn what he needs to know so that he can function successfully in our world, and that includes learning responsible behaviour. Being careful is an important attitude to learn and so is taking care of things. It teaches being a caring person.

If the child's skates are left outside, a natural consequence and discipline would be if the skates were put away for a day or two and could not be used. It is a way for a child to learn that responsibility goes with ownership, what we own needs to be cared for. When we do not take care of things we do not have them very long. If instead you ignored the skates and left them out there, the child would not have a responsible role model to imitate. The skates might be stolen and that would "teach him a lesson", but would it be what we want him to learn? We want the child to feel cared for, safe and protected, to learn about the world and to be a responsible person. If the child is without the parent model and parent caring, the child will toughen his armour, turn off his feelings a bit more, and diminish his humanness. That is not our goal for parenting. We want to help him learn.

It would be equally undesirable if the parent always put the things away, not involving the child and not allowing consequences. Then the child has no opportunity to learn responsibility. It is of course self evident that the expectations vary with the response of the child.

What is possible for them on one day may be overwhelming the next and parents need to be in tune with their child. We need to be aware of the child's response and the meaning of the experience, because a child will feel inadequate when given tasks that are too difficult physically. Just because he may know how to do something does not mean he is emotionally able.

Parents also need to teach about doing favours for people we care about. "They are your skates, but I'll help you out today by going with you to get them" or in some cases: "I'll get them for you" gives them a chance to experience willing helpfulness. Often the child is up to doing a task with you when he is not up to doing it on his own. That is part of being a child. My experience is that children also want to learn to do favours and when it is in their life experience they learn to do it quickly and with a feeling of delight.

Resolving conflicts

If two friends are fighting, a natural consequence could be that they are not allowed to play with each other for a specified period of time. It is helpful for children to learn that leaving a conflict situation is a good alternative, not the only choice, but a valid alternative. Children too, each have their own ideas of what they want to do and what they feel is fair. Conflict with friends is inevitable, and children cannot be expected automatically to know how to work things out fairly. Teaching that skill is yet another parent task: they need parental wisdom and life experience to learn conflict resolution. Help children be aware of how it seems to each person, help them put in words other solutions or clarify the rules for them.

Letting disagreements escalate does not lead to developing good friendships, nor does always demanding your own way. Social skills must be learnt. The length of time of a separation after a disagreement needs to be clearly stated so the child knows what to expect. A vague "until I say so" leaves the child feeling powerless and unnecessarily vulnerable, probably leading the child to resent the control rather than learning from the consequence. It is important to remember that children forgive and forget much quicker than adults: fighters one minute can be best buddies the next minute. An imposed separation needs to give them time to calm down, and miss being with the friend. If it occurs in the morning, it could be time away until after lunch. If it is in the afternoon it could be the next day. If the other child is a visitor in your home it could be fifteen minutes. There is no exact rule, you have to try and watch the result and decide the next time accordingly. If this is your first child remember that you, too, are learning.

It is important to allow children to experience the natural consequences of their actions. Parents often try to control their children's experiences so that the child can be spared dealing with unpleasant consequences, or perhaps to try to protect him from the consequences. The parent does not want the child to suffer the pain, (such as being without his skates) and out of that concern may come threats, bribes or manipulation. In reality the child needs to be able to experience the world, to learn to live in it and not be over protected or over controlled. Of course a child is not ready to handle all of the world's reality and cannot be abandoned by the parent, it is always a question of balance, neither too protected nor too much on his own. Parents need to maintain their focus on the child's tomorrow as well as today. It is not only the present outcome that is important, but also learning for the future.

Even when you have been clear about expectations, have followed the family rules and set a good example, there will still be times when problems occur. Children do test to see if the rules are still in effect, to see if they have grown past them. That is a good time to ask yourself if in fact the rules need to be modified. Children do grow, and as they grow we need to be giving more choice and responsibility over to them. Because they are testing does not necessarily mean the rules need to change, but that may be the case, and it is important to consider it. There will be times when children will just test the rules looking for reassurance that the consistency is still there. The parent needs to know and meet the humanness and needs of the child that are ever changing over time.

We must concern ourselves with the child's inner needs, desires and thoughts as well as family and social values. Children are not puppets with strings for the parent to pull, nor clay figures for the parents to mould to their liking. Nor do they exist to live out the parents unfulfilled dreams of their own lives. They are separate people with their own perceptions, sensations and reactions living in a reality, and they need help in learning to do that well. Children's inner traits are very important and are lifelong friends or enemies.

Most parents want their children to tell the truth and will probably tell their children that. When an unwanted telephone call comes and mother tells the child to say she is not at home, she is not teaching being truthful. She is teaching making up stories to avoid unpleasant situations. In the early years what we do in the presence of the child has much more impact on his learning than what we tell him to do, so we must be aware of what message our actions are giving. That is especially true when what we do contradicts what we say. The plea "do as I say, not as I do" is not likely to work.

Family rules

Each family needs to work out for themselves what the family rules will be and then live by them. It is important that these rules be practised by the parents. The rules need to be clear and consistent. Family rules need to be stated in the positive: "Put your jacket on the hook" rather than "Don't drop your jacket on the floor". The "don't drop your jacket on the floor" does not tell where the jacket is supposed to go and negative statements usually have a negative tone of voice that go with them. The child not only hears a negative about the jacket but experiences the parents' negative tone.

When we value the child's feelings and help him to be aware of the pleasant feelings of warmth, caring, love and harmony, as well as the unpleasant feelings of separateness and unkindness, we keep alive the feelings that are the source of morality. Rudolf Steiner, in A Modern Art of Education* states it clearly:

> If before puberty we have awakened the child's feeling for good and evil, for what is and is not divine, these feelings will arise from his own inner being afterwards. His understanding, intellect, insight and power of judgment are uninfluenced; he can now form independent judgments from out of his own being.

Making the right choices

If the child has been taught to please others and do what others tell

*Steiner, Rudolf, *A Modern Art of Education*, Rudolf Steiner Press. London, England. 1972. p200.

him to, he will be vulnerable to being misled. The child who has a sense of self, an inner awareness of right and wrong, will be able to be responsible for himself and make his own right choices. It is not only the immediate outer result that we need to focus on, but the inner development of the individual child. We want the child to grow to be a teenager who can confidently say, "I know" and be able to choose for himself. When the parents are consistent, provide natural consequences, use the Rule of Three, the child is given the beginning of a value system. He learns appropriate behaviour, then in later years he has some guidelines for establishing a value system of his own as he starts making his own choices. The child who discovers the consequences of being destructive in the early years is not likely to choose to be destructive in later life.

What we experience in our environment becomes an inner experience, a memory to call on. The tone of the environment becomes an inner tone, harmonious or discordant. Having lived in his early years with the idea that being destructive is not acceptable, that hurting yourself, hurting others or hurting things is wrong, a child will have values to refer to when invited by peers to join in escapades that can be dangerous or self destructive.

Discipline from parents will lead to self discipline, a valuable human characteristic. The number of possible dangers in the world continues to increase and children are vulnerable. We need to care for them and care about them; help them develop the inner strength to choose to say "no". Our goal is to help our children choose acceptable social behaviour for themselves.

As children learn to care for and consider others they experience an awareness of the world beyond themselves; an important part of learning to be responsible and responsive to others. Children also need to feel they are being responded to, and having clear and consistent expectations and guidelines is the responsibility of parents. Being consistent does not mean being rigid, consistency comes from reason rather than rigidity.

All of us, and especially children, grow when given understanding, when others allow us to experience the existence of our inner selves. Ultimately we do not need others standing over us, we need teachers helping us learn by standing under us, understanding and guiding our thinking and observations, allowing our individual talents to unfold, recognizing our feelings with understanding. Humanness unfolds with understanding.

When you find yourself standing over your children, remind yourself that they too have feelings, thoughts, and needs that are seeking a healthy way to express themselves and to be acknowledged. The more you are in touch with your own inner reality, the freer you will be to greet the self of another. When you know yourself, you are free to know others.

Chapter 8

Image or Reality?

Our personal likes and dislikes are individual feelings, not right or wrong, just different. I like strong, clear colours, a close friend likes pastels. Neither choice is good or bad, right or wrong, they are different personal preferences. The fashion world may declare we 'should' wear the colour that they have declared in favour for this year (remember to translate 'we should' to 'they want'). I may decide to wear the 'in' color, but that would be a conscious decision rather than a feeling or a liking. My choice might come from a basic need to be accepted, to fit in; that would be a different experience from choosing a colour because I personally liked it. Liking what we are doing is a pleasant experience and helps us toward making ethical decisions.

The way we feel about something, how we relate to it and value it, depends a lot on what it means to us as individuals; how it fits into our world, affects us. If you live in the city or an urban area and have a weeping willow tree the dropping branches can be a continual nuisance. Picking them up is one more task, as is having to bundle them so that the rubbish truck will take them away. You may decide it is a good job for the children and try to get them to do it. Don't be surprised if they resist. If you view the task as a nuisance, they probably will too. Children imitate and learn from their parents. They also learn attitudes. Giving children jobs to do that parents dislike doing is an invitation to conflict.

Caring for things

We all have tasks to do that need to be done whether or not we enjoy them. That is part of life. However, if you want your children to value caring for things, to be involved with you in the many tasks at home, it is best to have them join you in the activities that you feel good about doing so they can share that experience.

If you live in a rural area and your home is heated by a wood stove, or you have a fireplace, then you will welcome fallen willow branches as free gifts to help you kindle next winter's fires. They will be gathered up and saved; they will become part of the fire that warms your home when it is cold outside. You can value them as gifts of nature. You box them, or stack them, not to be hauled away, but to be saved for the fire when the weather turns cold. When children join in gathering kindling for their own winter fire, they connect with your feelings of gratitude and an awareness of the cycles of nature. They experience doing something that is meaningful and has a purpose that they can understand and will enjoy in the future. It gives them a personal experience of present and future and an introduction to the value of forethought and of planning ahead. It is not an abstract idea but a real life experience. When children understand the value of an activity and experience its real purpose in life, the meaning of the task is different and their feeling about it is different, too. Each of us instinctively enjoys having our life and deeds on earth matter. It helps, too, when activities can be experienced as nature's gifts rather than nature's nuisances.

Valuing nature

Inevitably, the less we live with nature and relate to it, the less we value it or understand it. When we do not understand or value something our interest in it is diminished as is our concern for it. That becomes a real dilemma.

The more we live with technology, the more familiar it is to us, and the more at ease we are with it, the less we think of our relationship to it. We may trust technology more than we do nature because it is closer to us. Some people go to the extreme of not trusting nature, and choose to value technology over nature. They seek to control nature rather than trying to understand her. When we devalue nature we risk losing our human value. It is important to recognize that tasks given to a machine are taken away from human activity. Calculators do our calculation, automatic off switches replace our conscious responsibility, electronic instruments translate a one finger melody into a complete performance. Human talents and skills may be left undeveloped while machines replace human musicians. When man makes tools he uses them to increase his talents and skills; when man builds machines he risks giving up his talents and his skills. Of course machines are of value as labour saving devices in our current society, but we need to consciously consider what we are giving up to them and decide if that is what we choose to do.

By preferring technology, people discount the amazing wisdom of nature and then celebrate the cleverness of man. It seems that the more technology advances the harder it is to understand and know humanness, ourselves, and each other. It is hard for moral development to keep pace with technological development. We have the capacity to do things that we do not have the wisdom to decide about. We do not know if doing them is healthy or unhealthy, human or inhuman. An obvious example is technology in medicine. It presents us with many choices and decisions that our grandparents were never confronted with.

There are powerful forces in nature that are frightening to most of us. We cannot control nature's power: hurricanes, earthquakes, tornados, lightning, thunder and floods. Some people become anxious when they do not feel in control. There are other aspects of nature that we cannot control either but we appear willing to accept. The sun rises each day at a predictable time and sets every day at a predictable time; the moon too – consistent and dependable models! There are gentle showers, balmy breezes, beautiful blossoms followed by delicious fruits and nuts, and fragrance of flowers and herbs, butterflies from caterpillars, birds, animals in an amazing variety, and us the humans. All of this is somehow created in nature.

It is sometimes difficult to know just how humans influence the rest of nature and how we all fit together. We hear about the greenhouse effect, water and air pollution, and know that somehow they are connected with us and our technology. Humans, animals, the world of nature and machines all exist in our world. How do we fit together, how do we affect each other? How does the growing child learn to meet his goal of becoming a mature responsible person in today's world? What do parents need to know in order to help this future citizen?

Looking beyond image

We need to try to understand how we fit into the scheme of things, how things affect us and the world around us. We need to know what the consequences are of the choices that we make. We need to know what reality is and what being responsible means. There is image and there is reality. There are outer appearances and inner reality. Once upon a time the appearance and reality were connected. If it looked like grass, it was grass; either alive and growing or dead. Now we have artificial turf and it is not alive, never was, does not grow, but is made to look like living grass. . . It does have the appearance of grass if you do not look too closely. I did see artificial turf being sprinkled once, hopefully it was to wash off the dust! Knowing reality is getting harder.

Once it was the case that a person running for a political office told the voters what he or she believed in and what his future goals were, and the voters made their choices based on that. Now elections are often run by image makers, based entirely on outer appearances with candidates saying what people want to hear. Office-seekers often say or do not say whatever the image makers suggest. The candidates are trained to perform, to say what polls find that people want to hear. Their human individualities, values and dreams are not accessible to the voters. We do not get to know whom we are voting for, we only see the packaged product.

PR, advertising and TV images also have an immense impact on human relationships. Many people set their goals, dreams and ideals based on the non-reality of TV stories, movies, and novels. Portraying an image has become a social expectation for many of us. We are told that professional success comes from wearing the 'right' clothes, that 'clothes make the man'. There are status cars, clubs, vacations and addresses. Being seen in the right place does affect some people's chances of achieving their life goals; that makes the search for reality even more difficult. Clothes at one time were a reflection of the inner reality of the person, were chosen to be the reflection of personal individuality, or the group identity of ethnic groups or tribes. Now clothes are used to create or promote an illusion, to give an outer appearance, and at times to camouflage the inner reality or lack of it.

Seeking inner reality

A society that focuses so greatly on image makes it difficult to know and value who we really are inside, where our feelings, dreams, talents, and ideals wait. Our individual feelings, dreams, talents, and ideals wait to meet that real part of another person, yearn to find that human contact with another and suffer when it never happens. People then go through life feeling an emptiness that needs to be relieved.

Why is there so much disenchantment in society, so much drug use, school dropouts and crime? I think it is because we do not acknowledge the real humanness in ourselves and in each other. When the 'image' of one person seeks the 'image' of another person there is no real human interaction in the deeper sense of humanness. Each person is reacting to the other person's image, rather than responding from an inner reality.

There are two responses in social communication: one involves *acting* out of your own individuality, the other is *reacting* to another person. When we react the other person is directing our response, our freedom is given up. Someone is rude to us and we tell them off. That is reacting. Acting out of your own self is a very different experience from reacting to others. If we go through life reacting to others and doing what others want we have little chance to be real. We need to constantly remind ourselves to be real, to be who we are.

How often do you really look at the person you are talking to, how often do your eyes meet in gentle recognition of each other? I am not referring to the training that is given in seminars for business management to maintain eye contact for power or dominance. I am referring to a natural inner desire to meet the inner reality of the other, the inner dream, feelings, ideas of your friends, your child – a moment when you are really there and you allow the other to be really there. How often do you consider how the other person is feeling, what this meeting means to them? How often do others meet you in that deeper meaningful way? Not often enough probably if your life is like the life of most of us. How often does your child experience this real meeting with humanness?

Nick Hobbs*, Tennessee Director of Mental Health, describes

---

*January, 1980. Keynote Speaker – Innovative Community Programs Conference. California Department of Mental Health, Sacrament, Ca.

'burn out', a phenomenon of our times, as feeling powerless, unable to use our creativity. I treasure the wisdom in those words. It is not the challenges in life or work that frustrate us, that wear us down, rather it is not being able to use our own humanness, our inner creative self. We 'burn out' our real humanness when our value as a human being is disregarded, our ability to be creative is not allowed. Too often we are expected to perform as a machine that is controlled by outer power rather than by our own human inner direction and ability. I think many of our social ills are a result of burn out in daily living.

Cooperation from caring

Parents may be so used to living with the power and control of others that they risk taking it as an acceptable way of relating and try to run their families that way. Machines do need controls because they do not have the capacity for self control, but humans have that potential inner control if it is recognized and allowed to develop. People please or try to please people who have control over them but they also want to please people whom they care about. Healthy human relationships come about when there is caring and cooperation, when we please people because we care about them.

Family dynamics and relationships have a very different feeling when the goal of each person is to have self control, respect each other, help each other, and allow for the individuality of others. Respect and cooperation enhance family harmony; control and submissiveness disrupt it. It is important to be aware of the fact that it is possible for people to have different ideas, different points of view without having to fight with each other. We really don't have to fight with someone just because we have different views or opinions, likes or dislikes. If we each act in a responsible way, allow for differences, and help our children learn to do that well too, the world will be a very different place.

Chapter 9

Nature, Needs, and Humanness

When we decide to be aware of the inner being of the child, to understand the personal needs of the child and value his humanness, we have a way to understand **who** the child is.

There are two general philosophies about learning: the 'empty vessel to be filled' theory, and the 'allow the flower (child) to unfold' theory. It is easy to understand how both theories have developed. The inner being, the individuality, does need to unfold, but the child also has to learn the social expectations of the society in which he is living; its history and goals and values need to be understood as well as how to survive in that society. The child's inner being needs to be allowed to unfold as he is guided by the parent and shown how to live in this particular place in this time in history.

If you are a pygmy parent living in the forest you will be teaching different skills and values than a parent living with 20th century industrial technology. The issues are different, the skills needed are different, but the humanness is the same. More primitive societies must know the natural world, settle where food is available and where they can find water or they will not survive. With modern technology that is no longer necessary and man can now live in places that previously were incapable of supporting life. Some scientists have even suggested developing space colonies as places to live in what would inevitably be a totally man created environment.

With society's technological advances, different life styles have emerged resulting in less contact with the natural world. Parents have less opportunity to learn about reality from the world of nature and less opportunity to give practical training to children about the natural world they live in. Living with the technological world does make it more difficult to understand the nature part of ourselves and our world, our human nature and our inner reality.

Since many of us are now denied the opportunity of understanding the world around us and ourselves by living with and observing the phenomena of nature, we have to find other ways of learning and understanding. We must use our uniquely human abilities to think about what we observe, think about thoughts, to use forethought and impulse control to modify our current actions for future gains, in searching for our own values and life's realities.

Knowing the whole person

One way to approach the complexity of each of us is to think about the individual differences between us, and the similarities. We are similar in our physical biological organism. Although there are remarkable variations in proportions, generally the parts and the whole are similar.

There is also our individuality. There is a word for it, it is "I". Only I can refer to myself as "I" and I cannot refer to you as "I". Only you can do that. We both use the same word, but we are talking about two different people. I can talk about your head and my head, your arm and my arm, but not your I and my I. In some theories of psychology the I is referred to as the ego or the self. In religion it is referred to as the spirit. Often the language comes together. A person may be described by one person as being a strong *individual*, another may characterize the same person as having a determined *spirit* or being a brave *spirit*.

Talking about a person's spirit makes many people uncomfortable. When someone has been through an experience that overwhelms them, we may say "their spirit was broken". Breaking the spirit is a way to describe the effects of brainwashing and cruelty. We do accept the word "spirit" as having a real meaning, but it has not been used very often in child development or in parent education. Perhaps it is seen as belonging to religion and therefore not to be intermingled in education. However, it is a real part of every human being, and must be considered in any attempt to understand wholeness and humanness. Although it is an invisible quality, it is manifested and observable in activities.

A team with spirit does more than just go through the motions of the play, they have a mutual inner connectedness, determination, an added resource. A spirited person is more lively, more responsive, has an added quality that leads us to think of her as unusual or outstanding. In the world of competition she would be considered likely to be the winner. The spirit manifested in effort gives a source of inner courage and energy to persevere. A person in touch with her own spirit has a gentle strength, a soft but bright light in her eye.

You cannot pour spirit into a child, but if it is recognized, it can unfold. It is the awareness of the spirit of a child that leads to the educational theory of "allowing the flower to unfold". An unfolding spirit, however, will not automatically know how to grow into a responsible adult in this time and place. That takes learning about the world, society, others' individuality and learning how to be in harmony with them. It is this aspect of humanness that leads to the idea of an "empty vessel to be filled".

If the spirit of the child, the *being* of the child is acknowledged and allowed, the child will not be an empty vessel. But in a way there is the vessel that will need to be filled, to learn how to live in the world at this time in history and in the place where the child is living. The vessel is the physical biological organism that we recognize when we see a person. The invisible part is the individual spirit of the person. We must recognize the spiritual part of the child as we guide her through life.

Needs or wants

Growing into a responsible adult in this time and place requires learning about the world, society, others' individuality and cooperating with them. Helping the child learn to find her place in the world while maintaining her individual needs and talents is a way of parenting that allows children to grow into creative, thoughtful, responsible adults. In every family there are the child's needs, the parent's needs, and often other family members' needs also. Recognition of every one's needs and learning to function as a harmonious family unit does not happen automatically. It takes thought, understanding, and awareness of purpose. Inevitably one person's needs or wants will interfere with those of others and conflict will occur. It is important to sort out a need from a want. A need is something necessary, required for healthy human functioning. We need food and liquid and air and warmth. Each of these we need in balance, not too little nor too much. We also need harmony with others and a sense of our own self. A want is something we desire, feel we lack, wish for.

A child who is swimming may want to continue swimming, but need to come out of the water. If the child's lips are blue and her teeth chattering she needs to get warmed up. The child wants to continue playing to continue the activity, but needs to come out of the water. Parents who can discriminate needs from wants will be able to make healthy decisions in the care of their child. The child may plead, "I want to stay in". The parent can respond with, "I know you want to stay in, but you need to come out and get warmed up". The parent can acknowledge the child's desires without agreeing to them. Then the child experiences a parent who is aware of her, making decisions for her out of her needs and in her best interest. The parent will be respected and then there will be a basis for cooperating. That is quite different from a parent saying "I don't care what you want, you will do as I say". There will be times when a child will resist with an "I don't want to" and your reply may be simply, "But you need to", or, "I did not ask you to want to, I asked you to do it". The clearer you can be, the less confusing it will be for the child.

Parent-child conflicts and the need for discipline most often occur when the child is doing or not doing what she wants and that does not match what the parent wants. Sorting through the different views and needs and finding ways to sort out responses can demystify this baffling part of parenting.

Some child specialists urge parents to 'do what works', but that limits us to doing what works for the moment and does not consider the long term consequences; tomorrow is not considered. That is similar to planting that garden of seeds without knowing if they are flowers, vegetables, grains or weeds and waiting until they are harvested to see what has been planted. Caring for a garden without knowing what you are raising would be laughed at by most gardeners, and nurturing unknown qualities in your children makes parenting an unnecessary gamble.

Understanding nature and needs

When we are clear about our goals and understand how to achieve them, we experience the immense importance of parenting. Although having children is a biological process, raising healthy human beings requires more conscious awareness of what we are doing. Parenting is important; our children are our future. Few of us would be willing to go into a new profession without some training, and although the biological process of having a child does not require special knowledge, the day to day care of a child, if it is going to be well done, does. It requires a basic understanding of the nature and needs of children. Part of the nature of a child is being active, moving, exploring, investigating the world, and we need to learn to direct that activity in a healthy safe way.

The young child has the inner need to explore and discover the world around him in order to be a part of it. Children learn best through their own senses and experiences. The child needs to establish a direct connection to the world through exploration in order to be able to feel at home in it. We need to provide a safe opportunity for the child to explore as a way to learn about the world. It is our responsibility to guide and allow for safe exploration.

The ways in which we assure the child's safety will vary with the temperament of the child. The daredevil will need to be given clear limits for her exploration. The shy, sensitive child will need encouragement and protection. We want to accept the nature of the child and help him find appropriate ways to meet the world. If we think of him as a piece of clay for the parent to mould we will miss the essence and mystery of the child. Recognizing the child as a unique individual, with a spirit, as a person destined to bring to earth his talents through his own personality, allows us to experience the reality of the child.

A child with a talent for music will blossom when given the right instrument that will allow the talent to unfold. If the parent instead wants the child to be a competitor in sports and ignores the child's talent for music, the undeveloped talent will struggle for expression and lead to dissatisfaction or conflict. We are who we are, and our inner self needs to be allowed to find its way into the world.

Developing trust

When the child is accepted as who he is, is cared for and protected from dangers, but allowed to explore where it is safe to do so, exploring new things becomes a pleasant experience. When he can leave his parents to explore his world, satisfy his own interests, then return to his parents and be accepted, he begins to experience his own journey into the world. His own interest in the world that he sees and his desires to explore it are accepted. We will remember the Rule of Three as we help him and guide him in his explorations.

Allowing his exploration with the parent's guidance is a very important basis of interacting with the world and others in a healthy way. It gives the child an opportunity to experience trust, separateness and connectedness, all vital aspects of a healthy personality. This apparently simple exploration is in fact a profound experience in a child's life. He is testing his world, probably without even knowing it. To venture away from the parent, explore his own interest, and be welcomed when he returns creates a pattern for approaching future life situations.

If his venturing away is met with disapproval, he will have to give up his interest to be in harmony with the parents, or follow his interest and give up the parents' acceptance. In fact a toddler cannot survive without the parent so he gives up his own personal interests. He learns he is not to follow that inner being. If that is a regular pattern problems will develop. Erik Erikson's theory of Eight Ages of Man* identifies the personality traits of trust, separation and rejoining that develop in the early years. From his work with healthy and pathological personalities it became clear that what parents do at this early age makes a difference in the personality development of the child and lasts through adult life.

Being able to allow guided exploration is a growing point for parents. As baby emerges into a separate person with separate inner directed interests the child is separating from the parent. This can be a difficult time for some parents. When the infant is totally dependent on us it seems to be easier to listen to, consider and provide for his needs. We feel his helplessness and we feel needed and that gives us a personal sense of value. When the child's interests lead him to move away and explore the world on his own, when he is less dependent on us and more his own person, new feelings arise in the parent. The reality of the child as a separate person begins to emerge. Some parents feel rejected or challenged at this stage of development. That is especially true if the parent wanted children so that someone would love and care about them.

Understanding that the child is beginning the long journey toward

*Erikson, Erik H., *Childhood and Society*, W. W. Norton and C., New York, 1963.

being a responsible separate person and that this is an early stage of that journey can put this current stage into perspective. The parents' role is beginning to change as the child becomes self propelled but the new role is just as valuable and important as the previous role. This exploring is an important time in the life of a child and will lead to his later style of meeting the world.

Setting limits

While it is important to allow the child to explore and experience the world out of his own inner interests, it is equally important to set limits to his activities so that he can learn that there are times when his desires must be inhibited because of his own safety or the desires or safety of others. The child needs a balance between the idea that his needs should be completely ignored and the idea that his desires should always be allowed. The permissive philosophy of child care does not help the child learn to value and respect others and this is an important concept for him to learn. It is as important to experience and recognize boundaries as it is to experience exploration.

Parents must have an ideal, a goal to aim for as they guide their child in the balance of his needs and the needs of others. If the parent gives the child the message that anything that he wants to do is alright he will have difficulty seeking ideals, truths and realities as he grows and develops. If he does not live with those ideas as he is growing up it will be a concept he may not think to seek for.

Being active is as natural a part of childhood as is having feelings and desires, feelings about physical needs (hunger, warmth, and comfort) and soul needs (being affirmed, cared for, and feeling safe). Parents must accept those feelings as a healthy part of humanness. Feelings need to be acknowledged, kept alive and educated. The world needs warmhearted, caring, concerned people who are in touch with their own feelings and the feelings of others. The common thread that binds people who abuse children, animals, or themselves is the absence of feelings; they are people whose feelings have died away. Sympathy, empathy, compassion, and morality are all based on feelings. You don't think guilty, you feel guilty, you feel love, you feel concern.

Accepting the feeling is different from accepting the behaviour that the feelings lead to. If we are able to separate the child's feelings from her actions and verbalize both, we have an immense advantage in teaching the child appropriate behaviour. If we remove the child, saying, "You want to play with the kitty, but it hurts him when you pull his tail", the child has learned about himself and the cat and you. In this simple statement he has learned an immense amount. He has learned that you direct his behaviour, that the cat matters and has feelings, and that you recognize his needs and his desires in a caring way. Then if you gently pet the cat and help the child learn how to do it properly, he will have learned the right way to express his feelings. He may not learn the first time, but if you respond in the same way each time, making his learning consistent, he will in time learn the healthy way to play with pets.

Teaching the child to be kind and gentle to animals is an important part of learning. What we think, the values that we learn, as well as how we feel, determines our behaviour. Behaviour makes visible what we think and feel. Behaviour can also be an indicator of the harmony between individual needs and the environment.

Need for acceptance

Children, as all healthy humans, are social beings and need to be affirmed. That is an important basic aspect of human nature. If we acknowledge each other and are aware of each other's inner experience we are accepting each other's reality, accepting that each of us is an unique individual. When our separate identities are considered and valued we are reassured. We inwardly experience that we have a place in the world.

Being excluded, shunned or ignored are all ways of depriving people of this basic human need. It brings about feelings of rejection, self doubt, perhaps shame, even pain. Advertising uses this reality to sell us products, to threaten this human need. They warn of the possibility of bad breath, body odour, not fitting in that will lead to a life of loneliness and rejection. They exploit these human concerns to sell their products. Having these feelings is a real part of being human, a basic part of our social human nature. When we use this knowledge to help in our parenting task, to help meet our child's needs, we are using the information in a creative and positive way. When the child calls out "watch me" she is verbalizing this need. Children need recognition and human interaction, they need to learn acceptable ways to give and get attention.

An important aspect of learned human behaviour is: future behaviour is determined by the response to current behaviour. If the child imitates our waving bye-bye and we are pleased by that he will do it again. The child given attention for what he is doing, will do it again. If the child toddles off and the parents run after him saying, "I'm going to catch you", the child will have learned that it is fun to run away. You may not have meant to teach that but in fact you did. Children learn from experience and interaction with others and they are learning all the time. Healthy children seek out pleasant experiences and want to avoid displeasing those they trust and care about.

Remembering the child's need for affirmation and that future behaviour is determined by the response to current behaviour, we have two valuable keys to understanding how behaviour is learned and an opportunity to teach what we want children to learn. These two aspects are intertwined and form the basis of the theories of behaviourists. Being aware of behavioural principles does not make us behaviourists any more than knowing what vitamins and minerals are in fruits and vegetables make us a vegetarian! The ways in which we use information are important.

We need to use behaviour theory to control our own behaviour, to be aware of how we are influencing the child, not as a way to control the child. A child does not grow to be a healthy adult when taught to be a puppet or a slave. Children need to be affirmed and will do what they need to do to be noticed. Even negative attention will be experienced as being better than no attention at all, better than being ignored and feeling that they are not acknowledged. This need to be affirmed is a healthy human need, it allows us to live in social groups and to be aware of each other. It is an important part of our human nature that needs to be recognized and allowed.

When we are aware of the child's need to be affirmed and we realize that the behaviour we pay attention to will be repeated, we will be wise to pay attention to the behaviour that we want to encourage. If we notice children only when they misbehave, we are inviting them to misbehave to be noticed.

If the toddler pulling the cat's tail had been yelled at, and hit for pulling the cat's tail, he would have been noticed for doing that. When he wanted our attention again, he would have that experience in his memory bank to call upon. If we had just ignored the behaviour, he would not have learned the right way to give attention to pets and although he did not get our attention he would get the cat's attention. Children need to learn and we need to help them learn what is appropriate. They have their feelings, their needs, their desires, and we need to show them how to meet those needs in a healthy way by directing their activity.

The way we act as well as the way children act is the outer visible response to how we feel and what we think. Doing things, being active is an essential part of being human. Doing what is caring and constructive, what brings joy and a sense of meaningful accomplishment, nourishes our sense of self.

Feeling is part of being human. Being in touch with our feelings and caring about the feelings of others are important models for children to live with. The parent's thinking about behaviour and how it is learned, and their caring feelings, can help guide the child to behave in an acceptable way. We want to recognize the child's unfolding self and help him learn about the world around him.

Chapter 10

Learning for Harmony

It may be startling to realize that everything that we know how to do in our world, we have learned. It is an amazing realization. We don't just know things, we have to learn them. We all have learned personal care skills, domestic skills, vocational skills, social skills and appropriate behaviour. All this learning makes it possible for us to live more or less successfully in this world. What we know how to do today we have somehow learned from someone in the past through imitation or direction or through discovery. It is an interesting experience to stop midway in a task and ask yourself, "How did I learn how to do this, who taught me? What else did I have to learn previously to be ready to learn how to do this now? What abilities were necessary and what learning was involved?" Hopefully we have not only learned survival skills but also skills that allow us to live in harmony with others.

At birth the infant has the ability to cry; that is her way of communicating and calling for us. She has the ability to suck, and the ability to move her limbs. At first the infant's movements are random rather than intentional and the parent has the responsibility of changing the child's position, ensuring that she is safe and comfortable. Nourishment has to be brought to her, unlike the baby animal our baby cannot move on her own and seek out food. A new born baby is totally dependent on us for survival, then slowly she learns how to ask us for help with her needs, eventually learning how to meet her needs on her own. The skills learned early in life become the basis for later more complex skills.

Society's ways

In the early years of childhood, learning through imitation allows the child to begin to learn our society's ways of providing for our needs. Little children love 'helping' their parents with daily tasks and it is a wonderful way for them to learn and experience the world. Being involved in what the parent is doing, seeing the parent caring for the home and the people in it, hearing about earlier times, old-fashioned times and what people used to do gives children healthy images of the past to carry with them and it is a natural way to learn.

Parents need to bring stories about life to their child. Before public schools, libraries, TV and cinema it was more obvious that storytelling was a treasured part of the culture. The elders told stories and legends to the younger people, stories that they had learned from their elders. Through storytelling individuals had the opportunity to inwardly visualize and share in the experience of the group. That is how traditions and wisdom were passed on from generation to generation. Learning to be a storyteller is a valuable talent for a parent to develop, and an event children will delight in. It gives them an opportunity to build up a storehouse of their inner reality about life and to learn human values. There are many steps needed in learning about life and hearing stories can help the child find her place in her family and in society. Learning comes from listening and watching as well as doing.

Chores are something that a child has to learn about. A child does not know how to cut the grass just because she is 'old enough to know how'. She learns how to cut the grass by watching others doing it and then later joining in and helping an adult. Then she can learn about the cutting and the trimming, the needs of the grass and how to take care of the tools that are used. You can make the task more interesting by telling her about grass as food for horses, sheep, and cows and the need for lawn mowers in places where animals do not eat the meadow grass. She will enjoy stories of how the horses waited while their masters visited the old Manor House, and the more visitors there were the more horses there were eating the grass. The more horses there were tethered at the house the larger the lawn became. Later people who did not have horses used lawn mowers so that they could also have the luxurious appearance of trimmed meadow grass around their home. All the lawn games that followed were possible because of the short grass created by the nibbling horses . . . When children learn the history of what they are doing they feel more connected with the meaning of the chore. The imaginative pictures that are created connect us to the world and nurture us.

When children have the opportunity to work with an adult to learn how to care for things, having a chance to observe and help, they gain a feeling of confidence about being able to take over the job themselves at a later time. The task will be familiar, they will have an understanding of how and why it is done. When children grow up feeling connected with the tasks at hand they have a better chance of being at ease with it. They learn not only skills but also attitudes as they watch those around them in the world.

Remember, if the child has heard you complain about the job and feels it has been given to her so that you do not have to do it any more, expect her to imitate the complaint too. If you have objected to the task, she will probably also object. It is a very different experience to take on a task because you have learned it and are ready to do it than to do a task you have been given because no one else wants to do it, or before you are able to do it well.

Observation

An important part of learning to care for things is learning to look at what you have done, see what still remains to be done, and know if it is done well. The focus needs to be on the task completed not on the person doing the task. It is a very different experience to look at a clean shiny table and value its appearance than it is to be satisfied with yourself for having done the job. The focus needs to be on what you are doing, not a judgement of you.

When a child makes something and says "that is not good" she may be thinking "I am not good". It is also possible that she is protecting herself by criticising the work before others do. If you are there at the time, you can look at what she is trying to do and ask "how can we make it better?" Then you will help the child focus on the project at hand. When things are not up to our expectations that means we have more work to do. Negative comments can become an undesirable habit, something we want to prevent.

Learning to care for things is more than just going through the motions. Swinging a broom on the floor is not the same thing as sweeping a floor clean. We have to look at the floor to see if it is clean. If it is not clean, then it does not help the child to hear that she is not a good sweeper. It does help to have someone look with her at the floor and see what else needs to be swept up. When parents approach the development of skills as a part of growing up it gives the child a clearer picture of her relationship to her parents, her role as an apprentice to functioning members of society. That will help her learn to be a functioning member too. The more skills that we have, the more comfortable we feel in the world.

Timing is important in teaching skills. The child needs to be developmentally ready to learn the task. Teaching what can be successfully learned is part of the goal, and the right timing is when the child is physically strong enough to do the job and visually able to discriminate the details of a successful outcome. When the child has had the chance to observe you doing the task, hear how and why you do it the way that you do, practise it with you, she will have had the opportunity to learn from imitation and direction. It is true that she could learn how to do the dishes or the yard from discovery, but that would inevitably include many frustrations along the way and probably complaints and criticism. It is important to allow discovery, but not to require it. It is an exciting way to learn about natural phenomena, but not a successful way of learning chores.

Realistic expectations

There is the old 'sink or swim' theory, but why would you want your child to sink? When a child is given a task to do that he struggles too much to achieve he has an inner feeling of inadequacy. Children trust that their parents would not expect more from them than they could do. When they cannot meet their parents' expectations they feel there is something wrong with themselves. It is not a pleasant experience to feel that you are not capable of the task that you have been given. It is a fertile ground for self doubts. Our goal is to help the child learn to be successful through imitation and direction. We want the child to feel competent, to develop a good self image and self esteem.

Helping children learn appropriate behaviour as well as skills for life is an important task of parenting; children have a great deal to learn in our world and it takes time. A child is not bad or dumb because she does not know how to do something that she never had the chance to learn. The more the child learns about the world and the more comfortable she feels about herself, the more responsible she can be. She has the basis for feeling self confident and for having a positive self image. The way children learn to behave is greatly influenced by the way they feel about themselves.

Self esteem

A poor self image can be the cause of chronic misbehaviour. The child who feels worthless, inadequate, and left out dislikes herself and what she is feeling. She will probably resist whoever or whatever is making her feel that way. The way people act is influenced by how they feel and what they think. The child with high self esteem who knows and accepts who she is, plays and talks and walks differently. Her inner feeling of security enhances her ability to interact with others and use her talents with ease. In *Your Child's Self Esteem** Dorothy Briggs views self image as the child's most important characteristic. We give children the opportunity to develop a good self image when we help them learn appropriate behaviour and life skills, accept their individual differences and acknowledge their feelings as real.

A negative self image is one cause of misbehaviour in children, they see themselves as bad. The child who hears that she is bad, learns to think of herself as bad, and then acts that way. Then she is likely to be scolded or punished, her misbehaviour is noticed and that will confirm her idea that she is bad.

When a child is feeling good about herself and feels accepted and loved, she does not misbehave. A paradox of parenting is: the more unlovable the child is, the more love and caring she needs. Love in the sense that there is someone in her world who cares enough about her to help her find a new way of relating to the world. She needs someone to remain connected with her and help her bring herself back in harmony with others. Punishment has limited value, it does not give a chance to learn and feel successful. A child who is misbehaving needs someone to help her learn new ways to relate to others out of mutual respect and caring.

We would all prefer to avoid the problem of misbehaviour in children. Life is more pleasant for them and for us without it. That is a wonderful goal but not a realistic expectation. It will help to

---

*Briggs, Dorothy Corkille. *Your Child's Self Esteem* Doubleday & Co., New York 1970

remember that the behaviour is mirroring self image. The child is acting out the way she feels. The child who believes that she is bad, acts out of that belief and plays the role that she feels is assigned to her. She mirrors the response of the world around her as she perceives it.

Solving problems

If negative behaviour and critical responses have become a family pattern, this can be changed by parents making a conscious effort to change the usual responses they make. The parent needs to help the child learn new behaviours that are acceptable. First try to understand how the child is feeling and what needs she is trying to meet. If you are able to discover what these needs and feelings are, then you can direct more appropriate ways to meet these needs. It may be a younger sister wanting her older sister's attention and not knowing how to ask for that. Instead she teases her, gets into her things, or tells tales about her to get her or your attention. You first have to discover what the problem is, what the needs are, before you can solve it. If you are unable to sort it out on your own, find a family or child therapist to help you. Any problem can be solved if the people involved want a solution. That does not mean getting people to do what you want done, it means a solution mutually arrived at.

It is important for parents to act out of their own goals, not simply react to the children. Remember, reacting to others puts them in charge of the situation, acting out of yourself and your own values and intentions allows you to bring about changes and direct your family's life. It is important for parents to consider their personal family goals together and to set the tone in the family. If things go sour, your goal will be to get them back in harmony. Find a caring way to intervene and redirect the behaviour. Look for what the child does that is right and comment on that. Give attention to appropriate behaviour. The child who feels worthless and hopelessly inadequate may seek out anti-social ways to confirm her identity. The child with a positive self image is rarely a problem child.

When parents are warm, caring, and confident in what they are doing they provide healthy examples of human behaviour in a relaxed way. The better our parenting skills are, the better we are able to provide the child with a chance to learn about the world and the people in it. Whatever the child experiences in her environment becomes a memory picture that makes up her individual life story. That will be the basis of her data bank of feelings and thoughts. We each have our own thoughts and our own feelings built out of our life's experiences and our reactions to them. No two of us are exactly alike so do not expect that from your children. They are not to be carbon copies, they are real live individuals. Watch them, get to know them for who they are.

We each have our own feelings, our thoughts, and our activities. These three influence the way we relate to ourselves and to others. In daily life the three become one and we do not use or see them separately. They blend together in harmony when all is well and that is our goal. Learning to live with inner harmony and in harmony with others allows us to develop our own individuality and fulfill our own destiny. It is as individuals with a sense of our real self that we can grow and discover new things about the world. Creativity is an inner experience that comes through individuals being given the opportunity to develop their own unique talents, the gifts that we each have. The more we experience and learn, the more we grow. The more interest we have in the world, the more interesting we are as people. When we feel good about ourselves and value the talents of others, then we have the tools for living in harmony with others.

Chapter 11

Affirming the child

A stressful time in many family's lives is late afternoon before the dinner hour. Dinner has to be prepared, perhaps the house put in order, and the children are under foot, wanting attention, perhaps squabbling with each other and generally being a nuisance. An understandable reaction is an annoyed "I'm busy, go and play". Although it is an understandable reaction it is probably not really going to solve the problem. The children may be tired and hungry, but there may be other feelings as well. They may have the feelings of being left out or ignored, of not being attended to. It is possible that they will follow your direction to "go and play", they may leave you alone and then go and fight with each other somewhere else – probably not quite what you had in mind!

Notice me please

When children feel left out, feel that the world is going on around them without being aware of them, they react in whatever way they have learned to get attention. Being noticed, affirmed, or acknowledged is a basic human need and being ignored is as painful as being hungry. It hurts inside. We all have the need to be recognized or affirmed, the need for others to notice us and pay attention to us. We also have the need to be accepted, wanted, valued; but the most basic of these needs is to be acknowledged, to have our existence noticed. By the time we are adults we may have developed a variety of defence mechanisms to protect ourselves from feelings of separateness, of emptiness. Most children are undefended, more vulnerable to their experiences. They react more openly and directly to what is happening in their world. They have not built up their defence mechanisms yet.

Being aware that most children will do whatever they need to do to get our attention, we will try to think about that as problems arise. Parents need considerable self discipline constantly to ask what the children need and how they feel, but it is the quickest way to healthy solutions. When feeling left out, alone or ignored, children will seek attention and instinctively they find that negative attention is better than no attention at all. Getting attention is an ego survival mechanism for a child, not something the child plans or plots, and when we are aware of this we can look for new solutions to old problems. If we are aware of this basic need, the need to be affirmed, then we can recognize in ourselves and our children when this need is not being met and then find a constructive way of meeting this need. When we feel separate or alone we feel excluded, uninvolved, and that is not compatible with our nature as social beings.

A familiar example is the parent talking on the telephone. Children feel that the parent's attention is not with them, that it is totally directed elsewhere. Most children have a predictable response of attention-seeking behaviour when their parent's ear and the telephone connect. It is almost uncanny how quickly they react to this event! The child's feeling of being out of the parent's consciousness can explain the misbehaviour of children in other situations too. Children seem to have an invisible radar that tells them they have slipped out of their parents' awareness. They use misbehaviour to express their need to be reassured, affirmed, cared for or noticed, to be included in the awareness of the person caring for them.

If they are behaving appropriately and no one noticed them, a subconscious need propels them to a behaviour that will be noticed. It is important to realize that it is a subconscious need and the child will be unable to answer your question, "Why did you do that?" If the person caring for the child has insight and asks the question "Were you feeling left out?" the child will then have a chance to get in touch with the feeling, he may then be able to acknowledge it. Of course, it has to be said in an accepting and understanding way, not with annoyance or criticism.

If children are only noticed when we are irritated or annoyed by what they have done, they will inevitably be involved in a negative interaction with us, and the child will feel he is a nuisance or bad. Out of the need to be acknowledged the child may continue to act in whatever way he has learned to get our attention, but it will be a

negative experience. Slapping or hitting tells the child that he is
noticed, but the child does not learn new appropriate behaviour from
it. There may be an improvement for the moment, punishment
usually stops the current behaviour, but the same situations will
reoccur again and again because the child has not learned a better
way of dealing with the experience.

Children's responses to negative interactions will vary: one child
will continue to be mischievous to be noticed, another child will feel
rejected and may withdraw feeling unworthy and unaccepted, and
yet another child will feel challenged to a power struggle. The
reactions will vary depending on the temperament of the child and
his characteristic way of meeting the world. The problem may
intensify or the child may go away, but mutual harmony will not be
restored. All children will benefit from our realization that they feel
the need to be in our awareness, to be a part of our world. Being
affirmed is an experience that helps us discover our personal values
and confirms our existence.

Sharing tasks

It takes some forethought on the adults' part to plan ahead to provide
a meaningful activity during busy times, but the rewards are great.
An activity for a toddler during meal preparation time might be
playing with some unshelled nuts, a large spoon, and a pan and a
bowl. Then they can 'play cooking' while mum or dad cooks.
Children learn about life through play, they experience the world
and their activity in the world. Learning through their own activity
is a natural part of child development.

An older child might set the table, as they get older they could peel
carrots, measure or count ingredients, stir – any task that allows
them to feel a part of the process. They are learning new skills,
cooperation and feeling a part of the family activity. It does take
some planning, maybe even more of your time, but if you value
harmony, it is time well spent. Young children love to help and
imitate what their parents are doing and what children learn from
imitation in their early years becomes their habits in later years.
Providing good models for imitation is the best way to help the child
develop good habits.

When children are helping they feel included and they have a positive experience. They feel productive and valued. Their need to be included is met in a positive way. They also learn living skills and the more skills we have the less vulnerable we feel. Feeling competent and self assured grows out of knowing how to do things and feeling useful.

Some children seem to be born with an interest in exploring the world and learning about it. For other children the world is more of a mystery and learning about it is more difficult. It is important to meet the needs of each child and be sensitive to individual differences. Learning chores is difficult for some children, easy for others. Some children need a lot of guidance, others less. Don't expect children to be able to do what you want them to do without being aware that they need help in learning. We are not all the same, we each have different talents and capacities and different learning styles and speeds. Because we want a child to do something does not mean he is ready to learn it.

Building self-esteem

Our goal needs to be to help the child to be successful, to help him gain new skills, to increase his feelings of competence and self worth. Children will generally try to please and do whatever we ask them to do, but when they struggle too much to meet parents expectations they feel inadequate to the task and have self doubts. Self confidence comes from being successful. These feelings become life long soul moods and affect the way we approach life.

It is important to be aware that adults also can feel inadequate when more is asked of them than they can reasonably do. Expectations from children or your spouse can trigger conflict and feelings of anger in you when the expectation is not easily met. It helps to be aware of your own feelings when you feel others are expecting too much of you. If you tell them how you feel it will help them understand you and themselves, and later in life they will better understand other people too.

When we provide meaningful interactions, show interest in the children's learning, and take time to include children in the daily activity of family life, we provide an opportunity for them to experience important human qualities. A chance to be part of a cooperating social group is a valuable life experience. If we want them to be considerate of others, we need to show them consideration. If we want them to be caring people, they need to experience being cared for as children. By being aware of our children and including them in our activities, we let them know they are valued and recognized for whom they are, a wonderful basis for gaining self confidence in meeting the challenges that will come to them in the world.

We need to make it possible for the child to experience in his life the qualities we want him to have as an adult. We have to give to the child, let him *experience* valued life qualities, before we can expect those qualities from the child. By remembering that the child's experiences in the environment are taken in, internalized and become inner traits, we put the right value on the child's environment.

Chapter 12
Calm Mealtimes

It may come as a surprise to discover that eating can become a power struggle between parent and child. How is it possible that a basic human need can become an area of conflict and how can we avoid that problem? As with all aspects of child care, if we learn to do it well from the beginning, life later on will be much more serene. It is not possible to overstate the importance of good beginnings.

Part of the history of eating problems goes back over 60 years to professional advice parents were given. As early as 1928 John Watson recommended in his then influential Psychological Care of Infant and Child* that parents should control the time of feeding their child, not based on the needs of the infant, but based on clock time. An arbitrary time schedule was to be imposed upon the child. Perhaps it was a big step forward in the mistaken concept that man is a machine. If the child awakened hungry and it was not feeding time mother was not to feed her until the clock on the wall said so. Nature's signals of hunger were not to be trusted. A lot of parents and children spent painful times together as parents tried to follow professional advice. 20 years later Benjamin Spock's Baby and Child Care* supported a more responsive approach by feeding on demand and he was labelled by some as being 'permissive'. How strange to think it is wrong to feed a hungry infant! At least now parents had some choice as to which theory to follow in the care of their children.

The choice was there, but it was not easy. They had to choose between two very different views and that inevitably brings up uncertainty. Parents had to ask themselves, "Is it right or wrong to

---

*Watson, J. B., *Psychological Care of Infant and Child*, W. W Norton and Co., New York, 1928

*Spock, Benjamin. *Baby and Child Care*. Simon and Schuster, New York, 1976

meet the needs expressed by my baby? "What about my instinct to care for this helpless little one?" Watson's focus was on controlling the child's behaviour; Spock's concern was for kind parents learning to care for their infant. That brings parents to an early decision about their role in relationship to their new baby.

Physiological/psychological needs

It helps to consider the complex task of the newborn infant. The baby has to learn to integrate being awake with eating and then sleeping in comfort. Before birth eating, sleeping and waking were not required. Suddenly these functions have to be developed. Alternating between sleeping and waking and including eating becomes necessary for the child's survival. That is a lot to take on all of a sudden. For those of us on a day time schedule we hope that the baby will choose night time for sleeping and day time for waking and eating. As tiny stomachs cannot manage that all night we have to put that hope on hold. If the child eats in a warm, calm, nurturing environment, and is 'burped', then we increase the possibility of her sleeping in comfort.

Another need of the newborn infant is to feel safe and cared for, relating to the psychological care of the infant. Of course we do not remember our early care, our experiences are not memory concepts that we can recall, but they continue to influence our relating to others and the world around us. Subconscious memories of the early meeting between the child and the world live on in our psyche, our soul. Our physiological and psychological needs are interwoven in eating. Nurturing, sharing, caring, or controlling, demanding, denying – all can find their way into meal times. The atmosphere and mood that accompanies meeting the physical needs of the child are of vital importance. It may not matter to a machine, but it does to a little human and it will matter more to some children, less to others, depending on their sensitivity.

In feeding, as in all aspects of child care, balance is the key. The extremes go from following the dictates of a clock on the wall that does not feel and has no connection with the child, to totally following the dictates of the child who does not have any awareness of the needs of the mother and father or the others in the family. Somewhere between those two extremes we need to find the balance.

It is clear that an infant has no awareness of cultural eating habits, nor of the family schedule. What the child does have, however, is her own feelings of hunger, fullness, interest in eating or disinterest in eating. Because the child has these feelings does not necessarily mean that we have learned how to read them.

Learning to read the child's needs is as important in feeding as it is in other areas of child care. Remembering that there is wisdom in the child and that we want to connect with it is always a useful guide. We need to balance the child's needs with the family's needs, find a way to bring them together. Children's needs vary and as they grow and mature their food needs, likes and dislikes will change. It is important to respect these differences and not expect all children to be the same or stay the same.

As individuals we each develop our own personal likes and dislikes which may change over time. Some people prefer spicy food, some sweet, some salty food. We each have our innate food preferences and parents may also have their socially learned bias. If the child dislikes chocolate we will probably accept her rejecting those 'treat foods', but if the child dislikes meat and we are a meat eating family that may be more difficult to allow. (For those who think these are extreme examples I hasten to add I'm describing the food preferences of my own sons: one at an early age did not like meat and another at an early age did not like chocolate. My grandson likes both of them).

Personal likes and dislikes

It may be helpful to look at your own reaction to food to gain some insight into how you feel about food, and then use that as a guideline to help understand others. Different people have different reactions, but we all have personal preferences. When we are not feeling well and are asked to eat food that we do not like, we can experience our body's rejection of that idea. Hopefully, you have been able to preserve that self awareness. If we are in a social situation, in good health, and we are served food we do not like we may be able to swallow it, but probably without pleasure. Of course we can repress our feelings, our inner reaction, and not experience them, but that is not what we are striving for. That is denying our humanness. If it is an exotic food that we have never eaten we will probably approach it cautiously at first, perhaps take a little nibble. If it is a foreign taste but not offensive, we may find it easier to eat with a familiar seasoning or sauce on it. It has been suggested that the world could be divided into two groups, those who love ketchup and those who do not!

Our likes and dislikes are real physical experiences that we can be conscious of. We can be aware of them as our own inner experience if we have preserved the ability to be aware of our own bodily responses. Unfortunately, some of us have been taught to disregard our own personal inner signals and then we are told what is the 'right' way to feel, or what we 'should' like. If we believe in relying on mechanical thermometers, over-load switches, barometers and the like, how can we ignore the most amazing creative sensors in our own bodies? Is it because they are not man made that we believe they have less value? We are again at the roots of why parenting has become so difficult even when we want to do a good job. We have been given so many scientific concepts, live in a increasingly man-made world, and live less and less with a consciousness of the wonders of nature that we have reduced our experience of it. It is another example of the more scientific theories we acquire, the more difficult it is to understand nature and humanness, our world, ourselves and each other.

We can observe animals living in nature apparently knowing what to eat and when, without any nutritional studies or concepts about it. In fact zoo keepers try to learn about and replicate the natural instinctive diet for the animals in their care. They trust that the animals will naturally choose to eat the food that is healthy for them. Some of us have grown up with so many outer directions and expectations on our eating that we have lost the sense of eating what we need when we are hungry and stopping when the hunger is satisfied. We have been tyrannized by "eat everything on your plate" and "be thin". No wonder it is confusing.

Avoid eating wars

Eating is not often enough an inner directed natural experience any more. Our physical state affects our psychological state, and our psychological state affects our physical state; eating is connected with both. Many parents, especially nursing mothers, do respond to their infant's expression of hunger and allow the body's expression of need to influence feeding time. Somehow we need to find a way to blend the child's individual expression of need and our own family's eating customs while trying to preserve an awareness of the child and integrating that into the family unit. What we clearly do not want to do is develop a power struggle over food or give it a meaning that it does not really have. Eating is not intended to be a tool of coercion, of pleasing or displeasing others.

If the child is taught to eat to please the parents, she is given a weapon to use when she wants to annoy them and she loses the sense that eating is something that she does for herself. The need for healthy food is an individual bodily need and the child needs to learn that and to be allowed to experience that.

Remembering that the young child imitates those she lives with and has a natural desire to please her parents, we have the ideal time to establish healthy eating habits. In the early months of introducing solid foods, we see parents instinctively using this awareness. The parents put the spoon to their mouths, express pleasure sounds, and then offer it to baby. The mood is established that a pleasant event is occurring, behaviour is given to imitate. It is an experience to share, not a power struggle.

A very different experience and interaction occurs if the parent holds the child's head, forces the spoon in her mouth and makes her eat. It is fair to ask how we would like having this done to us? Making the spoon into a flying ship that zooms around and then lands in the child's mouth is not what eating is about either. Although the parent has good intentions, tries to make eating a happy time, it distracts the child from enjoying eating. Parents will need to help with the feeding when the baby first needs solid food and is unable to feed herself, but it needs to be done without giving a performance. It is possible to feed the child without force when it is a pleasant experience and the child is ready to eat. It may involve two spoons, one for you and one for her. That gives the child a chance to be involved, to practise feeding herself, while you ensure that she has enough to eat. She will enjoy being involved even though she is too young to feed herself completely. She will have a chance to imitate and practise, develop a new skill and grow towards the goal of learning to do for herself what the parents at first have to do for her.

Presenting healthy food

Three meals a day is traditional in our society. At work that may be expanded by coffee breaks. We even have special names for the three meals: breakfast, lunch and supper. Even if we don't eat them, we are likely to say, "I don't eat breakfast", or "I skipped lunch today", still giving validity to the concept of the three meals, whether we eat them or not. We don't expect a baby to abide by that custom, rather we recognize her need to eat every three or four hours. Because the toddler is on solid food does not mean she is automatically ready to switch to these three meals. Young children need mid morning and mid afternoon snacks, and probably a bedtime snack, perhaps of warm milk with honey. Structuring those healthy snack times helps to avoid fussy times and is a helpful plan. Anticipating the child's needs and providing a special time for them gives the child the feeling of being cared for and a sense of security. If the child's needs are not planned for, then the child becomes hungry, fusses, gets in trouble perhaps and life is then a bewildering experience. Our goal is to have healthy meals and healthy snacks at a regular time presented in an attractive way.

A sandwich cut in quarters makes it easier for a child to eat. Apple slices are easier to manage than a whole apple, orange sections are easier than a whole orange. A centre of raisins with radiating carrot sticks will appeal to most children. An apple sliced horizontally has a lovely star in the centre. Banana rounds filled with peanut butter make a novel snack sandwich. A tasty pineapple yogurt drink (⅓ glass of plain yogurt with pineapple juice stirred in to fill the glass) with crackers will be another treat. It is important to give small quantities to little children so that they do not feel overwhelmed by the task at hand. If it is tasty, attractively presented, at a regular eating time and you have not made eating into a power struggle, the snack or meal will be enjoyed and the child will eat what she needs.

When the world of the child is consistent and predictable she can more easily fit into the family structure. Little bodies have an immense amount of growing and developing to do and the child's nature is to be moving and active; all of that requires a regular supply of food. Expecting little children to eat large quantities less frequently just is not realistic.

The pitfalls are many

Unfortunately, it is all too easy to be influenced by what friends or relatives say, and then you can lose your own natural insight. When we give up our consciousness and awareness of the child and the child's responses and make ritualistic demands, the pitfalls are many: "Sit there until you have eaten everything on your plate"; "If you don't eat it now you will have it for the next meal"; "You cannot have dessert until you eat your vegetables", "You cannot go out and play if you don't eat"; or an angry "Eat your food". I hope none of these sound familiar to you. Then there is the other extreme of withholding food, "You're a bad girl, go to your room and no supper for you". The pitfalls are many.

Most of us know the old saying, "You can lead a horse to water, but you can't make him drink". We can also be certain that if the horse is feeling well, the water is safe, and if the horse is thirsty, he will drink. People will, too, if their instincts are allowed. Human behaviour of course is more complicated than animal instincts and it is not the intention to oversimplify complex situations. However, we do need to be aware of what natural advantages we have on our side and how we can best use them.

Expecting the child to sit in a chair at the table while she is eating is realistic and an important beginning to a pleasant meal time. It also avoids spills and messes in other parts of the home which can be an unpleasant experience for everyone. If you start off with the expectation of eating at the table, both meals and snacks, if the adults set the example of sitting at the table when they are eating, then this imitated behaviour becomes a habit and will be accepted by children as the natural way it is done. If each person has their own regular place at the table, this is another bit of helpful structure for the child. The more consistent and predictable life is for the child, the clearer it is for her, and the easier it will be to learn.

When the child developmentally matures so that it is possible for her to sit comfortably for fifteen minutes, only then is it reasonable to expect her to sit at the table that long at meal time. There are many aspects to appropriate behaviour at meal time. It is another family experience that lends itself to basic values. Children need to learn to do it carefully, to treat each other with dignity and respect, to share, not grab but ask for what they are unable to reach. They need to learn to be aware of each other, not to interrupt or intentionally annoy anyone. It is another opportunity to communicate and relate with human dignity.

Eating with gratitude

We can expect the child to sit at the table and we can expect appropriate social behaviour, but only at the level the child is capable of. When we present the food in an attractive caring way, we set the example of eating with pleasure and gratitude. By starting the meal with a grace or prayer of thanks to the earth for its gifts, gratitude to the people who made it possible for us to have the food, and to those who prepared it, we give the child important human concepts that she needs words for.

If we present the meals in this way and we have accepted the fact that the child will also need healthy regular snack times, then our anxiety about the current meal being eaten can be reduced. If we are relaxed at meal time we will have a better chance of making it a pleasant time. With an awareness of the human need to eat food to nourish ourselves and maintain health, we are better able to nurture the child. We are thinking about the child's needs, not how she can please us.

If the child hears us say, "I really like that rice, thanks for fixing it", or "that juice was just what I needed", then she will begin to have those pleasant thoughts associated with meal time. If instead it is a rushed affair and she hears, "why did you cook that?" or "you know I hate that", she will be learning that too. I am not suggesting being a pollyanna, but I am suggesting there is great value in talking about what is right rather than what is wrong, and modelling gratitude for the meal that is served. When you see something that is wrong, that can be your trigger to look for something else that is right and comment on that. That is a skill that serves us well as parents, commenting on what is right. It helps, too, if parents have an awareness of what food is and why we need it, and that will take some thinking about. When we eat we take in something from the outer world and make it our own. It is a very individual and personal thing to do and yet a universal thing. It is not true that "we are what we eat", we are not a combination of peas, apples and potato chips. A lion is still a lion even if he eats lambs. What we eat is broken down, destroyed and transformed. The substances are then recreated by some amazing mysterious process into our own body substance, warmth and energy. When we think of eating as a natural process to provide nourishment for health and activity we have the best chance of handling the meal time in a successful way. It seems self evident natural, healthy foods without chemicals, poisons, or artificial additives will be more easily eaten and transformed in a natural way. By avoiding power struggles, demands, and manipulations, and by valuing food for what it is, we help children grow in awareness of eating as a natural human experience.

If you are not conscious of why you are eating, it is not likely that you can give your child the right feeling about meal times. The fruits of the earth have been created to nourish man. Living food is needed to sustain life. Food is also needed as a source of energy and warmth. Our bodies are biological organisms (not machines) that regenerate themselves by some wonderful natural process. To intrude into this wonder of nature and turn it into a unpleasant power struggle or technological debate creates false concepts and unnecessary tensions. A healthy happy child wants to eat healthy food.

The vast number of theories about nutrition, health, and weight control validate the idea that the process of eating is a mystery. It is sad to note the current increase in the mental health problems related to eating. Anorexia nervosa and bulimia are examples of acting out social-emotional problems through eating. The victims punish themselves and their families and the world at great cost to themselves. The anorexic distances herself from the world, rejects it or tries to have power over it by not taking in food. The bulimic devours the world without self control and then feels guilt or anger and gives it all back by purging herself. The obsession with being thin contributes to the problem, but it is certainly more complex than that. The issues of control are ever present. The focus on image rather than reality strongly influences many menus. For many looking thin is valued above being healthy. There was a time when the image of a very thin person represented a greedy miser like Scrooge or a heartless and wicked witch. Bones were not the only part of the human body that was valued. Being a lean, mean machine is a new idea. When eating is recognized as a natural process to provide nourishment and we don't introduce power struggles and criticalness into meal times we have the best chance of helping children eat in a healthy way.

Avoid rewarding with sweets

Children as well as adults need a variety of healthy foods and that includes some sweets. Fruits are a natural sweet and can be served fresh, stewed, baked, or as juices. When natural sweets are a part of the meal they are less likely to be used as a weapon. Telling a child during a meal that she cannot have a dessert unless she eats the meal is an invitation to disaster. It distracts the child from the food that she is currently eating and focuses on what will be happening later. That prevents her from experiencing the present moment and also brings about feelings of powerlessness. It introduces a problem that was not there, and that makes meal time unpleasant. It calls the child's attention to, and overvalues, the dessert. It implies that the dessert is more pleasant and desirable, but not available for her. At some level of consciousness we are saying that we are not giving her something that is important to her, but we can ask ourselves why would we do that? If we do this frequently we will be establishing a habit of focusing on dessert and taking away from the main part of the meal.

It is possible to have healthy sweets. Flavouring vegetables or rice with sweet and sour sauce, adding fruit or fruit juices to vegetables and grains can provide food that is welcomed by the child with a sweet tooth. If cookies and cakes are an inevitable part of your family life, it might help to have them as a mid-afternoon snack. Having a structure for eating sweets may be a helpful way for you to avoid using them as coercion. We want to provide an environment where the child enjoys eating health-giving food with a feeling of pleasure and satisfaction, celebrating with gratitude an understanding of the nature of man.

A food that a child hates one week can become a favourite food at a later time, if we allow that to happen. New foods take some getting used to and children's tastes develop and change. We want to allow for that without turning it into an unpleasant game. A helpful family rule can be that everyone takes one bite of whatever is served. That allows for introducing new tastes and foods without overwhelming the child with demands. If a child has allergies, obviously that has precedence over a family rule. It also helps to avoid comments about "good eaters", "big eaters" and "little eaters". We don't want to judge eating just as we don't judge breathing. We also take in air from the world, but I have never heard a parent comment about "poor breathers".

Enjoying eating

With the goal of doing what is right for the child, caring for her so that she can experience a harmonious relationship to the world, we recognize the child's needs and feeling about eating and respect them. By preparing food in a caring way, serving it in an attractive way, we allow the child's own interest to be directed to the food and allow for an experience of pleasure. The concept that food that is enjoyed is more easily digested is easy to accept. By providing healthy food at regular intervals we allow the nature of the child to direct her own varying needs.

Eating is something that we do for life and lucky are those who learn to eat in a healthy reasonable way, celebrating life. Using food for emotional needs or wars puts food in a sphere where it does not belong. Learning good habits early, eating healthy food in the right amount is a good basis for a healthy body. When a child has had the opportunity to eat out of her own needs she has gained a valuable lifetime habit.

Chapter 13

Happy Bedtimes

Is bedtime a part of the day that you and your children enjoy and look forward to – or dread? Bedtime is another daily occurrence that can stress an otherwise happy home. When parents come to me exasperated by the family night wars, I immediately wonder if they are lacking a predictable, consistent bedtime ritual. The usual bedtime complaints include the child refusing to go to bed (resisting), having a nightly temper tantrum (acting out), or not settling down. The less confrontative child may keep calling for extras: a drink of water, a favourite toy, the light on or the light off. The list can be endless, limited only by the discomfort and resourcefulness of the child.

The Need of Ritual

If we really listen to the child, we can hear his inner wisdom telling us of his need for ritual. Young children need to experience their world as predictable, they need their world to be consistent. One way we can provide for this need is through structure and ritual at bedtime. Consistent, predictable events are the foundation of a peaceful bed time. The child who feels calm, peaceful, cared for and safe has the best chance of accepting sleep time. The parents' challenge is to make bedtime a delicious event.

Pleasant memories and moments we enjoy attract us and are the events in our lives that we look forward to and want to repeat. We try to avoid unpleasant experiences, and so will children. If bedtime is unpleasant for you, it probably is unpleasant for your child, too. The good news is that since you are the grown up, you can change it, and by changing the way bedtime is approached you can change your child's response to it. The obvious secret is to find ways to make bedtime a pleasant, special memory, a caring finale for the day. Needless to say this puts demands on the parent to have forethought and self discipline.

For those who think that children "should" just go to bed when they are told to, remember to translate that "should" to "I want". Some parents tell me that they just let their children fall asleep whenever they want to, wherever they are, and later carry them in to their bed. The problem that grows out of that is when the child wakes up at night and cries, the parent has to go in to calm them back to sleep. It is not surprising that it would be disturbing to go to sleep in one place and wake up in another. The deeper concern is that the child is not learning how to go to sleep on their own and at some age that will no longer be acceptable. Probably the problem of bedtime is just being postponed and then old habits will have to be unlearned before new habits can be learned. Most of us wake up at night at times, but have learned how to go back to sleep. With adults, if that is not the case, we acknowledge that we have a problem. Sleep researchers have found that children that fall asleep elsewhere and wake up in bed are more likely to wake up crying at night. By filming children through the night they have observed the difference in children who wake up, resettle themselves and go back to sleep and those children who wake up, look around and start to cry.

The miracle of sleep

Your own ideas associated with bedtime will inevitably affect your approach to this time of day. If your own bedtime is a pleasant event for you and you have pleasant feelings about being able to relax, leave the world of conscious self activity and awake refreshed to meet a new day, then you will have an appreciation of sleep that you can convey to your child. The miracle of sleep is not something that most of us spend time thinking about, even fewer try to understand it. We expect to wake up feeling rested, and if that does not happen we feel that something is wrong. It may be easier for us to be aware of the lack of restful sleep than it is to wonder at waking up refreshed. Given a bit of thought we realize that sleep is a mysterious gift of the Gods. Where does our conscious self go when we are asleep? How is it possible that we can wake up feeling rested, renewed, with energy to complete the tasks that we were too tired to do the evening before? If *you* go toward sleep with gratitude and wonder, you have a better chance of creating a delightful experience for your child, a pleasant ritual to end the day.

When sleep for you is an escape from the day, and sleep for your children is your escape from them, it is more likely that you will approach bedtime with an attitude of duty; just one more thing that you have to make your child do. I assume it is self evident that you can't make anyone go to sleep, the most you can do is provide the environment in which this amazing phenomenon can occur.

Relaxing in comfort

The physical environment is important, too, for comfortable sleep. Clutter, a room that is too hot, too cold, too light, too dark are all things that can make it more difficult to get to sleep. A bed that is too small, a lumpy mattress, uncomfortable pyjamas, all make it difficult to relax in comfort.

Soft, smooth cotton sheets that are gentle to your skin, and warm flexible cotton and wool blankets that respond to the body's warmth in a healthy way are the basics of comfortable sleeping. Added joys are a lambswool mattress pad and a goose down pillow. Then you can bring thoughts of the people on the farms that grow the sun ripened cotton, the people that care for the gentle lambs and shear them, images of the dignity of the goose, the skills of the spinners, and weavers that make the sheets and blankets, thoughts that allow for true human connections in the world of plants, animals and man. Living with comforting, relaxing thoughts at the end of the day, having a chance to be aware of and grateful to others, the many people that we never see or meet, but whose work make our own lives more pleasant, brings us a mood compatible with sleep.

Learning about the world they live in is one of the tasks of childhood, and for those who do not live with the growing and making of the things they use, they need stories to learn about them. When children do not have the opportunity to experience and discover the world as it relates to them they can feel isolated and unsafe. Parents can bridge that distance with stories of other people, plants and animals.

Synthetic materials do not carry the same stories, connections and realities. They may be cheaper or easier but they do not come to us from the wisdom of nature, the caring of people, the wonder of the natural world, and generations of people passing on the skills involved. Synthetics do not absorb, interact and relate in the way natural substances do. There is no pollution or toxic substance connected with natural substance.

When parents tell me that their child has a high body temperature, or gets hot easily, I immediately wonder if they are wearing synthetic fabrics or have synthetic fabric sheets and blankets. Often when babies wear synthetic outfits you can observe the child perspiring, while the hands, feet or back of the neck are cold. Synthetics act more as barriers than natural coverings, they do not absorb moisture and do not breathe the way natural fabrics do. Once you have experienced the difference yourself the choice is an easy one. How much easier it is to get in a bed that you love and that welcomes you, connecting you with the world of nature.

Transition to sleep

No matter how wonderful the bed and how pleasant the thought of the bedtime ritual, there may still be a problem of the transition from waking activity to nourishing sleep. A child on his own cannot make the transition from full speed ahead to peaceful relaxation in bed. Young children out of their own nature live in the present and are all absorbed by what they are doing. As adults we have learned to think about future events and past events, we can be doing one thing while thinking of another. That is not the nature of a young child. When the child is in the moment and the parent is planning the future, the two are out of rhythm, harmony is gone. It helps when the parent is aware of this, joins the child's world, enters the child's activity and leads him to the new activity. If the child is playing with cars and it is story time, suggest that Mr. Car Driver come to the sofa so he can hear the story you are going to read, then allow time for that to happen. That way of relating is very different from a stern "Put that car away or you can't have a story". Be aware that the parent is the one who has the responsibility of being in charge and structuring the events although it is based on the child's needs. The bedtime ritual needs to be parent directed, based on the needs of the child.

There is no intention of putting the child in power, children need their parents to be responsible for family rules and rituals and to direct the daily routine of the home. We do not want children growing up feeling they are in charge of the family and responsible for it. It is not healthy for the child to be intimidated by parent power nor for the child to feel that he can tell everyone what to do. It is equally harmful for the child to feel omnipotent, as it is for him to feel like a victim of a power struggle. A child needs to be cared for to grow up feeling safe and protected. The child who makes the rules and takes on the role of parent misses the nurturing experience that allows for feelings of trust and being cared for. If the child is acting as if he wants to be in charge it is a reminder to us to get back to our job of parenting, caring for the child. We need to take back the parenting responsibility of directing the daily schedule and helping the child learn.

In the early years parents establish patterns for their children that become lifetime habits, so giving thought and consideration to what you are doing will bring years of rewards. Being responsible parents, caring for your child, includes providing him with a pleasant transition from activity to rest and sleep. There are many natural rhythms in our life and sleeping and waking is a daily one. Since we do it every day of our life, it certainly is important enough to learn to do it well.

Each family will have their own ritual worked out around their own life style. It is having the consistent sequence of events that makes the difference. If the sequence is started at an early age and the parents are consistent it will become a habit that the child will live with. The child too will anticipate the sequence of events, and will have healthy habits to incorporate when he is old enough to manage his own bedtime. Power struggles rarely appear when rituals are faithfully followed. It is when the child feels uncertain that the need to test arises, to explore if the rules have changed and to see what extras are available and who is making the rules today.

Value of ritual

The value of ritual is that it gives us a connection with the past and makes the present predictable. The more predictable a child's life is, the easier it is for him to learn what happens when. I hope by now it is not necessary to state that we want the predictable events in his life to allow him to feel safe, cared for and protected. Parenting means doing what is right for the humanness of the child. The ritual needs to be an experience that allows the child to feel safe, to be able to trust that what is happening is right for him.

The successful ritual could start with putting the toys away together for the night while the parent talks about each thing having its own place and needing to go back there. Then a leisurely bath allowing enough time to play with water toys. Perhaps you want to open the windows in the bedroom to air it out during the bath time. After the bath hanging up the towels together, wiping up spills, and putting bath toys in their own place. Then perhaps a snack, brushing teeth, toileting and off to the bedroom. Next closing the curtains or shades, putting a favourite animal or doll in the bed, for the luckiest children lighting a beeswax candle, and then in bed for a quieting, relaxing story. After the story a child's prayer or blessing, snuffing out of the candle, a goodnight hug and kiss, and the thoughts of sweet dreams, wondrous stars and the time to get rested, to grow, and to become strong.

When this is a nightly ritual, that means the same sequence every night, going to bed will have a special meaning and will be a predictable meaningful time for the child. Giving the child this form and structure has a harmonious effect. It adds to the child's feeling of being cared for and protected by the parents and provides an environment that encourages sleep. When the process is consistent, very soon the child will know what comes next. The child and the parent will both be thinking about the same next event. They will be in harmony. What is familiar and expected does not need to be talked about or directed, but happens as a familiar routine to all concerned. There is no conflict when pleasant predictable experiences occur.

It is important to note that child care at any time is not something that will work by going through a routine because someone told you to. Real caring for your child comes from a relationship, a desire to know and experience your child. Children need to relate, they are relaters by their nature. Adult cleverness, power and manipulations do not work in the long run. Children grow up, they don't just get older and then automatically know what to do on their own. What they are doing now they have learned from you, whether or not you intended to teach it. What they know when they are older they will also have learned from you.

If you have a ritual, but find the child is asking for extras, take that as a cue, do yourself a favour and include those extras in the nightly routine. Perhaps it is a drink of water, then make certain they have one, or have a glass of water by the bed. Anticipate their needs and ensure that your ritual meets their needs.

Fear of the dark

Many children become fearful of the dark and sleep is unlikely to follow if the child is afraid. Have a nightlight, leave the door open, close the closet doors and window shades to avoid shadows in the room. Perhaps a flashlight by the bed will be reassuring. Some children feel safe with a favourite animal that they pretend or believe will protect them. Remember, your goal is to have sleep a welcome comfortable event of the day, a pleasant natural occurrence. If you have a pet, help your child be aware of how they stretch, relax, sleep, and look so contented. Value sleep for what it is, a time to be refreshed, relaxed and renewed, and your children will too. It will be important to remember that we can expect children to go to bed at the regular bed time, remain there and be quiet, but we can't demand that they go to sleep. Sleep comes, it is not ordered, so we prepare for it and allow it. As with all aspects of caring for our children we present the patterns, help them with each step as long as they need our help, and then allow them to do on their own what they are able to when they are able to. Our ultimate goal is that children will learn to put things away on their own, take care of their personal hygiene, and get enough restful sleep to be a healthy human being. By showing them that we care about them when they are young we give them the possibility of caring for themselves as they grow older.

Bedtime problems

Parents will have to choose how they will respond to needs after the final good night. One choice is for the parents to go to the child's room if the child calls. The rule is clear, once in bed you don't get out without permission, but the parent when necessary will come to the room. The down side of this plan is when you finally can sit down and rest at the end of the day you may have to get back up again. I believe this choice is less likely to get out of control so on balance is worth the possible interrruption. The other choice is the child comes to find you wherever you are and asks the question or makes the request. The down side of this plan is you have the question to deal with, plus the task of getting the little one back to bed, plus the pattern of getting up after being put to bed. If you are going with the choice that the child stays in bed, then you go to the room to see what is needed and next day you change the ritual if you see the need. In my experience that way provides a better outcome.

Of course it is important to try to understand what the child is feeling, and discover what the child is thinking if there are bedtime problems despite your efforts to make it a pleasant experience. If the child has allergies, he may not be able to breathe easily lying down and that makes getting to sleep difficult. Perhaps older children are still up and the younger one objects. The older children can be asked to do quiet activities that are less disturbing and the younger child told he needs more sleeping and growing time now and when he is older he too will have a later bed time.

One way to decide when is the right time to go to bed is waking behaviour. If the child has trouble waking up in the morning, he probably needs an earlier bedtime. If the child can't get to sleep for hours after the final goodnight perhaps he is being asked to go to bed too early. This is assuming that the child has had a ritual that allows him to feel peaceful and calm. If the parent reads an exciting story or talks about the exciting events of the day the child cannot be expected to relax and go to sleep no matter how tired he is. Going to bed at 7:00 and to sleep at 9:00 will inevitably bring on unpleasant moments. No child I have ever known is able to lie in bed and relax for two hours without bothering his parents.

If the child is not asleep within 30 minutes of goodnights the schedule and the ritual need to be re-evaluated. Perhaps waking the child earlier in the morning will help, perhaps nap time needs to be phased out. Sleeping needs change as the child grows and also as the seasons change. Ritual refers to consistency of sequence of events, not to clock time. Be aware of the child's needs and establish your schedule around that. It is not likely to work though if you move the schedule up one hour on the night you want to go out or watch a favourite TV show. Our biological organisms do best with rhythm, and regular meals and regular bedtimes provide for this. When you go to bed at the same time each night you will get sleepy at that time and that is helpful for the child's bedtime rituals. Sleep comes when we are relaxed, the sense impressions of the daytime activity are dimmed and we feel safe and comfortable; then we are prepared to sleep. The more aware we are of preparation for this daily event, the better our chance of success. When bed is a comfortable cosy friend that enfolds us as we snuggle in, we will enjoy being there.

Chapter 14

Listening to your child

It is rather startling to realize the many things we need to think about, to be conscious of, in caring for our children; especially the everyday basic human activities of eating, sleeping, and also talking. Since talking is such a common occurrence, it may seem like a spontaneous thing that children do without our needing to think about it or be conscious of it. We may expect children to talk, to just do it; it may not occur to us that it, too, is a learning process. It will have to be first heard, and imitated, and then practised.

Communication through words

Speech is a unique aspect of humanness, a sacred gift from the spiritual world. It has been reserved for humans, a purely human capacity. Animals have sounds, machines have noises, and humans have speech. Humans can also make noises and sounds but machines and animals are limited and don't have the use of language that humans do. Some birds can learn to imitate words and echo them, but that is a very different activity than individually using words to express inner thoughts or feelings. With speech we can use words to communicate to each other what is happening for and inside of us. Words make it possible for us to have awareness and understanding of each other.

Because we have that capacity does not mean that we always use words in that way. Words can be misused to hurt each other. We see all of these misuses daily and have become so used to them we may miss seeing them as a corruption of the original use of words. Words rightly used allow for the highest level of communication. Speaking to each other makes it possible for us to bridge our individual separateness.

Before learning words the infant communicates with her parents through sounds of crying and cooing, and also with smiles, a silent but profound way of relating. When baby is first learning sounds it is a natural response for us to repeat those sounds to her as a way of acknowledging our ability to relate to each other in common babble. Speech is learned very slowly at first. Sounds are repeated, then combined and become words. We can observe that the complexity of learning to communicate with speech is a longer process than learning to walk, run and climb.

The toddler, when first learning to speak, wants us to repeat what she has said, she waits for us. It seems to assure her that we really understand what she is saying to us. She seems to have a desire to bridge our separateness through common words and understanding. It seems to give her delight and joy. The child's first task is to learn to name things, to learn the words for the people and the things that she meets in the world. Then she learns to talk about what the things are doing, what is happening, or what she hopes will happen.

Speech is learned from hearing words often enough to be able to imitate them and then have the chance to practise them. The child who speaks incorrectly wants to speak correctly and needs the experience of hearing words from us in the right way. When we respond with words it is important not to talk "baby talk" to the child, but to speak in a clear and natural way. It is demeaning to children for us to speak to them in "baby talk". They seek to learn from healthy models. This is another event that is learned through imitation.

Communication Through Listening

Young children usually chatter away with whatever enters their mind, they love to practise their new words and they want to include others in their world. It takes some learning to modify that, to learn that everything we think does not need to be said out loud. Learning to hear about the other person's world is important too. We all have to learn to be listeners as well as talkers.

Listen to your children when they speak to you. Words of wisdom come from very young children. Give yourself a chance to hear them and to get to know them. If you listen, really listen, to your child when she is young you will establish a lifelong interaction. If you want your children to talk to you when they are adolescents listen to them when they are young. If the process is not established in the early years, you are unlikely to be able to bring it about in the teen years.

A child who is listened to will express her needs and wants and will not have to act them out. God gave us words so we would not have to use our hands, fists, and feet to let others know how we are feeling. Being social beings we do want others to know how things are for us. When you listen attentively to your child as she is speaking, she learns to listen in that way too.

There will be times when you cannot listen and this is also important for children to learn about. Sometimes we have to wait. When you are busy with a task that takes your full attention, it is better to let your child know that you can't listen just now. You want to hear what she has to say but you will have to do that later. When you are occupied and can't listen, explain that to her, and ask her to wait. That is much better than the child talking when you are half listening. When you are involved in a task and your child is talking to you, you will probably feel annoyed and not be able to take in consciously what she is saying.

Be prepared for her to learn about this from her experience with you and include it in her repertoire of human behaviour. Sometimes she will tell you that she can't listen just then. Remember childhood is for learning and she may or may not be using this new concept correctly. Consider if she is using this new interaction appropriately, don't automatically object. If it is appropriate allow it, if not help her understand why it is not appropriate. It may not come at a convenient time, but be aware that she is trying out something new that she has learned from you.

Knowing when you are listening to others and when you are not is an important awareness to develop. Listening is a crucial part of communication. To listen to another we have to stop our own thinking to make space for the ideas and thoughts of the other. A valuable family goal is to create a space of peace between us, space that is a reservoir of goodwill and allows each of us to speak without fear of being attacked. When we disagree we can draw on this reservoir for acceptance and work toward understanding.

Listening skills are not easy to develop, they take time and practice. Have it as a goal, not an expectation. Try to set a good example for children to learn from. It is helpful to define for children when they need to stop talking and listen to others. It is better to say: "it is your turn to listen now" rather than "stop talking". Again we want to tell the child what to do, not what not to do.

An important part of communication is knowing how each other feels. It is important to be aware how our words affect others, and to be aware of how we use words, particularly with our children. Learning to speak politely with consideration for others is a lifelong task. It is not true that "sticks and stones can break my bones, but words can never hurt me". Harsh cruel words do hurt. It is not alright to hurt others, not even verbally. It is important that we model respectful communication.

"I" Messages

Two words that require our close attention are "You" and "I". Substituting the word "I" for the word "you" can have a profound effect on communication. "You" messages are often judgmental, sarcastic, or at least annoying. They make people defensive. When we say "you are being rude" or "you are thoughtless" we are finding an indirect and unclear way to express our own feelings and experience. When we translate "you" messages to "I" messages we say more clearly what we really mean and feel. If we change "you are rude" to "when I am talking to your grandmother, I do not like to be interrupted" we are describing our own inner experience. If we rephrase "you were thoughtless" to "I do not like to find the towels on the floor, please hang them up on the towel rack", we are telling the other about our inner self. It is true that whatever words are spoken tells more about the person speaking than the person spoken to or spoken about.

If we develop a desire for harmony in the family, a respect for others, then the children will want to monitor their behaviour to maintain harmony. If we instead tell them they are not up to our expectations (rude or thoughtless) they will feel rejected and may need to defend themselves or devalue what we have said. It is these seemingly minor differences, subtle differences, that make the difference in how a family relates to each other.

We discussed in Chapter 4 the value of rephrasing "you should" to "I want" to give clearer messages. When we give clear straight messages we communicate how we feel and think and that gives the other person the opportunity to reply with their thoughts and feelings. Practise listening for your own "you's" and find a way to change them to "I".

Perhaps your "you should not say that" means "that hurts my feelings". Or it may be "I cannot handle that just now". The clearer we are with our words and the more we use them to reflect our individuality, the better opportunity our children have to learn the right use of words. Also the better opportunity we have for living in harmony with others. If I acknowledge my feelings and thoughts and accept your right to have yours, I will want to hear what you have to say.

Understanding Through Words

We can try to understand another's experience, but it is only by exchanging words that we can confirm that we are really understanding each other. We need to exchange words so that we can confirm that we have an understanding of what the other person thinks and feels. We need to use words to verify, clarify, to confirm what the other person is telling us about herself.

Speech is a remarkable human gift and we need to remember to use it appropriately. In remembering that I am an individual being and that you too possess that individual essence we honour words that allow us to know that aspect of each other. If we think we know what the other person wants or thinks and we respond out of what that is, we are often heading for a misunderstanding.

If you put your words to my feelings or interests and interpret them incorrectly we are not relating in harmony. We are not only separate, but we have misinformation. You may be describing or responding to what you think is true, but if it is not what I think is true we are not having a common experience. We need to be able to use our own words to express ourselves. As we speak we need to be aware of the person to whom we are speaking, and when we listen we need to be aware of the person speaking. Speak to each other, value what the other person has to say. It is generally true that when people cannot talk to each other they talk about each other. Talking about people rather than to them is a spinning of wheels. It does not allow life to move on.

A conscious speaker chooses words with care and values the gift of speech as a link for healthy human relationships. Communication requires a listener as well as a speaker, an active listener and a conscious speaker. An active listener not only hears the words, but also tries to understand them as they are said and what they mean to the person who is speaking. We cannot really listen if we are thinking about what we are going to say next.

Speech can be misused to bring about confusion, to overwhelm people, to hurt others, or to impress others with how smart we are, how much we know. Georg Kuhlewind* describes speech as the ability most misused by man, and states that because we do not know what words are, we do not know what humans are. This is an idea of great importance and one worth exploring further. Speech rightly used unites people with each other and with higher ideals and realities. Speech has the potential of uniting my individual personality with your individual personality. Human speech is more than remembered words. The parent is not the ventriloquist and the child is not the puppet, dummy or robot.

For clear communication and to show respect for the individuality of others we need to be conscious of how we use speech. We need to speak out of our inner self and to the inner self of the other. We need to be that role model for our children so that they can learn real communication. We want to keep alive the treasure of free speech, the right to use speech freely, to know and understand each other. We do not want to ask children to say the "right thing" or what others want to hear. We want to help them to learn to put their own thoughts into words in a polite, considerate and responsible way.

If as parents we maintain our awareness that each of us has our own personality and individuality, our soul and spirit, that will help us in making it possible for our children to learn to express their own thoughts and feelings, needs and ideas. It is not always easy to put our inner feelings into thoughts and words or to ask for what we need, but it is important to learn how, and the family is the place to learn and practise.

*Kuhlewind, Georg. From Normal to Healthy. Breat Barrington, Maine, Lindisfarne Press. 1988.

Truthful Words

As we strive to be open for communication, strive to use speech in a kind and gentle way, a considerate way, we also need to strive to say what is true. TRUE. There is a word that philosophers have pondered for centuries. I am deeply grateful to the work of the Austrian Philosopher-Scientist-Artist, Rudolf Steiner, for his clear thinking and understanding of Truth and Reality and his life's work of helping other who seek it.*

His concepts have helped make it clear to me that there is a larger reality beyond me and my task is to seek it as clearly and as completely as I can. I may never see the whole reality, but if I know that it exists beyond me and I keep searching for it, that attitude will lead me closer and closer to reality.

It is important for parents to be careful to use words that are true to the reality that is being talked about. We need to communicate truth and reality and help our children to learn to do that, too. Commitment to the truth and the search for truth is a powerful bond for human relationships. Being able to believe each other is a basic need in family life. Without it complete trust is not possible.

If you feel that your child is not telling the truth then you have the task of sorting out what is happening and why. The idea is not to blame, but to understand. Putting her in the "bad girl" category will not be helpful. Accusing the child of lying will not help you to understand the problem. You need to be aware of what the child is feeling and try to understand the struggle. Has something happened that she knows you will not approve of? Does she want to avoid a negative reaction from you? Can you moderate your response to make it possible for her to tell you what really happened? Can you tell her that?

Perhaps she is describing an "I wish". She may be saying something that she would like to be true, inventing reality because she does not want to disappoint others. Is it a "just pretend", a moment of fancy that the child is wishing happened or wants to happen? When you are concerned that what you are hearing is not true then you can help the child by asking if it is a "pretend ", an "I wish" or a "too hard to tell about". Reassure her that she has

---

*Steiner, Rudolf, *The Philosophy of Freedom*, Anthroposophic Press, New York. 1964

permission to put into words what really happened, what she is worried about or fears. Help her to tell you what she needs or wants. Allow her speech to reflect her personal self. Let her know that you will be there to help her with the problem.

When she sees that you are able to face unpleasant or unwanted outcomes, that will help her learn that it is alright for her, too. Life is not always the way we would like it to be. We make mistakes, hurt others and damage things. Facing it takes courage, but the courage will come if you support facing issues. Be who you really are so that she can be who she really is. Trust her, believe her, and let her know the importance of being able to believe each other.

Children have an uncanny ability to know what we do not want to hear about and often they will respond to that unspoken message. Be aware of the non-verbal messages that you are sending. It is essential that you be open to hear what is happening. If you do not want to hear about a problem, chances are that you won't, at least not until it is a really big problem. You risk not knowing about it when the problem can be handled, only later when it is out of control. Reassure your child that you want to share the problems of living as well as the joys.

An important pitfall to avoid is asking a child if she did something when you know she did. That is a cruel set up, an attempt to catch her being bad. If you know she did something wrong, tell her and work out what the consequences will be. A child who feels she is being tested or tricked will not feel trusted and will not have good models to imitate. Also be aware that there are advertisements and unscrupulous people who use words to manipulate how you feel, think and act. They will promote ideas to influence your response. That is where you call on your sense of truth to help you be aware of trickery and deceit. It is important to tell the truth and also to recognize the truth.

Excuse Me Please

Truthful words listened to with respect create the basis of healthy human communication. We strive for that as adults, we do not expect it from young children. It will be our goal and we will help them learn it. Consideration for others in speech may require putting our own thoughts on hold until the other person is ready to listen.

When two people speak at once neither one is heard properly. There was a time when "children were to be seen and not heard". That seems extreme to most of us today so we need to teach children when it is alright to talk and when it is not. Teaching children that it is polite to say "excuse me" before they speak when others are speaking is an important first step. If they need to say something important to someone who is talking about another subject, "excuse me" will help them learn an awareness of and consideration for others. They need to learn not to interrupt when others are talking or if it is urgent to speak, to excuse themselves first before interrupting. It is important for parents to show their children the same respect. We also need to set the example of not interrupting.

It is customary to say "excuse me" when we feel we are interrupting, breaking in to another's thought when we have a different subject to talk about. It is not so clear though when we are talking to each other about something and you want clarification from me about what I am saying. Or perhaps you want to make a comment or observation about the same topic. In real communication it is an exchange of ideas, a relating to each other, both of us actively listening and talking. In real conversation we both care about the other, we are conscious of the other and interested in their ideas. Having a dialogue is different from listening to my monologue. If we are exchanging ideas and I say sharply, "Don't interrupt me" it does not feel as if we are really having a conversation. It feels more like I am giving a lecture; lectures and sermons do not enhance human communication. This is a subtle awareness that we have to develop. It is a verbal dance. If we are aware of each other we will be able to feel if we have cut the other person off. To wait to speak only when the other is silent is stylized avoidance of interrupting and leads to a feeling of disconnected conversation. We need to develop the sense for I and Thou.

Different Views

Yet one more area of possible verbal conflict comes when we have different views on the same event. This is especially true for children who are working out their differences. If the focus is on who is right, or who started it, we are headed for trouble. If we accept there are different points of view and different needs we will be on our way to finding a solution. The concept of different points of view is difficult for young children. It can be made understandable through an ancient Indian Legend*.

It was six men of Indostan
To learning much inclined
Who went to see the elephant
Though all of them were blind,
That each by observation
Might satisfy his mind.
The first approached the elephant
And happening to fall
Against his broad and sturdy side
At once began to call:
Bless me but the elephant
Is very like a wall.

The second, feeling of the tusk,
Cried HO what have we here,
So very round and smooth and sharp
To me 'tis mighty clear
This wonder of an elephant
Is very like a spear.

The third approached the animal
And happening to take
The squirming trunk within his hand
Thus boldly up and spake:
I see, quoth he, the elephant
Is very like a snake.

The fourth reached out his eager hand
And felt about the knee,
What most this wondrous beast is like
Is mighty plain, quoth he.
'Tis clear enough the elephant
Is very like a tree.

*Saxe, John Godfrey *The Blind Men and the Elephant*, McGraw Hill, New York, 1963.

The fifth who chanced to touch the ear
Said, even the blindest man
Can tell what this resembles most
Deny the fact who can.
The marvel of an elephant
Is very like a fan.

The sixth no sooner had begun
About the beast to grope,
Than seizing on the swinging tail
That fell within his grope
I see, quoth he, the elephant
Is very like a rope.

And so these men of Indostan
Disputed loud and long
Each in his own opinion
Exceeding stiff and strong.

Though each was partly in the right,
All were in the wrong.

It is helpful to consider how much more we can know about life's events if we look at them from more than one perspective. The real truth is the whole picture. We each have our own window on the world and when we combine ours with others then we come closer to the truths in the world. It becomes clear then how important it is for each of us to put into words our own individual experience to combine them into the complete picture. We are each a part of the puzzle and when the parts connect we have the whole picture. Words help us to put the picture together so that we can each know more than just our own perceptions.

By being aware of speech as a God-given gift to humans, and a way for each of us to express our own inner dreams, ideas, thoughts, and feelings we will have the best chance of using speech wisely ourselves and helping our children learn to do that, too.

Chapter 15

Growing socially

It is an ongoing lifelong task for both parents and children to mesh individual development and social development. There is my self, the other's self, my needs and the other's needs. Maintaining my sense of self while recognizing your sense of self will lead me to healthy human relationships. The usual daily schedule of regular events brings families together and provides for time of social learning. We can add to regular events some special events such as the playing of games.

Practising For Life

Games provide a natural way for children to learn about life; they are social interactions with clear definitions, rules, and boundaries. They give us a time when we can all know the same rules, we can learn that what others do effects what we do and we can see that the other players have their own goals. It provides a setting for each person to use their own skills while being aware of the others. Such awareness of others does not happen automatically, it is something for parents to help their children learn.

Learning about games and the art of playing them is another tool for parents in their role of helping children learn about the world. *Games are a metaphor for life.* Games are played best between children and adults when the adults help the children learn the rules of the game and also help them improve their skills. It is not a time for the parents to prove their superiority over the child, nor to be in competition with the child. Beating a child in play is not a desirable way to increase your own self esteem.

How parents play the game with their children is also a metaphor of parenting styles. If the child does not know the rules of the game and the parent tells the child what to do at each move that will be a very different experience for the child from playing the game knowing the rules himself, choosing to follow them and thinking for himself. Learning to make his own moves and own choices in games is good practice for later choices in life.

When someone else tells you what to do and you follow their directions you are not using your inner self and developing your own talents, capacities, and powers of observation and thinking. Learning about life through play is natural for children. Using games to give them the opportunity to think for themselves about what they are doing and learning to observe what others are doing is valuable practice for life. Games have an important role in childhood and they are an excellent way to practise healthy social interactions.

Game time is a natural time to enjoy each other, to learn to talk politely, to take turns and to follow the rules. Through games children can learn about winning and losing and how to do both gracefully. The primary goal is to learn to enjoy the social aspects of games and realize that in our current world sometimes we win and sometimes we lose. A useful social skill for children to learn when they win is to say to the others, "thank you for playing with me". Those are words that parents can use and also remind their children to say to others. Children need to learn friendly words and they learn them most readily through imitation. Help them learn to say "it is your turn", rather than giving the order "move". It is a natural time to teach considerate speech and friendly interactions. Remember that just because you have taught it once, twice, or twenty times, does not mean they have learned it. You need to keep on teaching until it is learned. Eventually we want each person to be aware on their own when it is their turn and we will strive to teach that.

The Value of Rules

All games have their own specific rules that need to be followed by all who are playing the game. To enjoy playing games together each person needs to know the rules and have the skills to follow them. To be a meaningful social experience each person needs to be aware of the others and share the common knowledge of the plan of the game. It is a wonderful way to learn at an early age that "doing your own thing" does not lead to harmony with others or to good social interactions.

If each person made up their own rules and did as they pleased it would not be a common experience, there would be no group experience, but there would be conflict and chaos. Group rules are necessary for harmony to be possible when individuals are doing things with others. To function socially with others requires the ability to give up our individual ideas and needs and consider the group needs and ideas. This is an important part of social learning that can begin in the home. It will develop skills that the child will use later in other places. Different games have different rules and that also enhances the child's understanding of predictable variations in life, the variety of life that we find in the natural world.

If you are playing draughts there is one set of rules, Chinese Chequers has another, and chess still another. All are board games, each involves moving pieces from place to place, but each has its own goals and rules for playing and winning. In draughts it is capturing the other pieces, in Chinese Chequers it is getting to a new destination, in chess it is making it impossible for the king to move. They are generally similar, but specifically different. It is a good way for children to experience the variables in life.

There are some rules that are universally the same, and there are other rules that are different at different times and in different places. There are the rules at home, the rules at school, the rules in stores, the rules in others' homes and the rules in church. There are also different rules inside and outside of each of these places. We are not born knowing that, it is social behaviour that we can learn if someone is willing to teach us.

Experiencing Differences

My experience in working with many children has shown that children who have not had the opportunity of learning to play a variety of games as young children have more difficulty being flexible and adjusting to new life experiences in an open confident way. They have missed that opportunity of learning to observe, take in the new situation in a new way and learn about it. They are likely to say, "this is just like . . .", lacking the ability to look at the new as a fresh different experience. No game is just like any other game just as no person or event is just like any other. There are similarities of course but there are also differences.

The similarities in games are that we take turns, follow the rules, move only our own pieces, and let others move their own. We have fun playing the game but not at the expense of others. The rules of play will be different, the board may be different, and the pieces will be different. In card games many different games can be played with the same cards and there are also games with special cards. Experiencing all this helps the child accept new experiences with equanimity.

It is more difficult to learn about the world, people and new games if you start out thinking that it is "just like" everything else. Your ideas of the old game get in the way of the new game. It is hard to make a fresh start. Thinking you already know about something allows a tone of arrogance to creep in, an "I know it all" attitude. In life that interferes with learning and with social relationships. Unhappily many children think that they are supposed to know it all and are criticized when they don't. That is not the message that we want to give.

We need to be aware that there is much to learn in the world and we want to help our children experience the wonder and joy of learning. We want to convey our understanding of the process of, and need for, learning. No one can know how to play a game until he has had the chance to learn it, not knowing how does not mean that he is dumb, it means he has not yet had the experience of learning it. When a child declines to play because he does not know how, tell him that you will help him learn. Play some practice games with him until he learns the rules. We want children to have the opportunity of greeting the new and the different with interest. It is valuable to realize that in life there are similarities, but that there are also important individual differences. It is helpful too in avoiding prejudices. Machines turn out things that are "just like" each other, but that is not what we discover in the world of nature.

Enjoy the experience

With the young child it is helpful to pick a game that the child has an equal chance of winning, a game that involves mostly chance. It is another time for you to help the child learn about the world and how to act in the world of today. Be aware that you are being the role model for the child and be sure that what you are doing is what you want him to be doing. It is as undesirable to lose on purpose to make the child feel equal to, or better than, the parent as it is to be in competition to win so that you can feel better than the child. The parent's role is to follow the rules, enjoy the experience and social interaction and help the child successfully learn and improve skills.

Learning the ways of humanness and the joy in caring social interactions is the aim. Caring social interactions deepen human relationships, competition does not. This is a good time to consider my thought about brotherly love. It is "Are you willing to have less so that others can have more, and are you willing to do more so that others can do less?" It is also important to ask: "Are you willing to have more so that others can give and are you willing to do less when others want to help?" I believe these are important social questions to consider. What do they really mean for your life?

Real life has some successes and some failures. It is valuable for the child to learn that there are people who want to help him when he feels that he is not succeeding. If a child knows that his family want to give him the extra help that he needs to be successful, this will encourage him to ask for help. When he experiences help from others it becomes an inner experience that he can later give back to the world. What is in the child's environment again becomes an inner quality, becomes a part of his personality that he can later bring to the world out of himself.

Fair Play

There are times that you may want to change some rules in a game, and then it is important that you make the changes before the game starts. In general rules need to stand and be followed, but on the rare occasions when they are changed this must be with prior common agreement in a way that is fair to all. It is not alright to change the rules in order to give one person an advantage over another.

For example, a child may want to continue batting in cricket until he is out, although it was previously agreed each child could bat for ten balls. That is not fair play and supervising adults need to see that the same rules apply to all. There is always the risk that a dominant child will make rules to his advantage and the disadvantage of others. This is an early experience in which they can learn about the importance of equality, another value among people who have respect for one another. Children have an inherent desire for fairness and we want to help them keep it alive.

When young children are playing games together the parent needs to be there to supervise and assure that the players understand the game, are clear about the rules and play fairly. Young children need parent or adult supervision to help them practise social skills. If left to settle their own disputes, to work things out for themselves, they will do it at the only level that they know and so the stronger will often end up dominating the younger or weaker one.

That is one of the differences between the animal world and the human world. Dominance and submission are natural in the animal world. Fairness and consideration for others need to be part of the human world. Consideration and fair play need to be experienced to be learned. When older children are playing with younger children it will be necessary for you to supervise their play until you feel assured that the older ones will be considerate of the younger children.

As the children grow older and develop their own sense of fair play, when they have learned to value the harmony of positive social relationships, then it is no longer necessary for the parents to be involved. They will be ready for the chance to work things out for themselves and learn to settle their own disputes. Even then there may be times when you will need to intervene to help them work things out fairly, but generally they need the chance to learn to work it out for themselves. First the parent directs the interaction and after the child has had the opportunity to practise then the child is ready to do it on his own. The parents' role keeps changing, as children grow. They need to experience life and then practise what they have learned on their own. Parents go from teacher to superviser to consultant.

The Urge to Grow

For civilization to progress we need to pass on to our children our learning, our values and our sense of morality and ethics. Hopefully, we will have provided opportunities for them to experience and value the good, the true, and the beautiful which will provide them with the basis for making their own ethical choices. Then they will need an opportunity to go beyond our teaching.

Real social progress means growing, developing and understanding. The urge to grow and develop is present in all of us. Developing skills and talents recognizes and nurtures that inner urge. Teaching values during games honours our inner spirit. Without values, respect for others and concern for our common needs, societies become decadent. Healthy societies are healthy because they have high social and human values, they acknowledge ultimate truths. Games offer the opportunity to practise for this human growth.

The adolescent's struggle is to discover both "who am I?" and "how do I fit into this world?" Games provide practice for life by developing skills and talents and learning fair play, knowing the rules. When we know our own talents it helps us define who we are; when we know the structure that rules provide and how to be fair we have good tools for fitting in to the world.

If an adolescent has had the experience of seeking personal goals with social harmony, then he will have a better chance of seeking out how he can use his talents in the world, rather than being out to see what he can get from the world. He, too, can be inspired to make the world a better place to live in. Knowing that we have skills and talents and an opportunity to be productive in the world brings optimism and enthusiasm to life's journey.

Games give the chance to develop skills and talents, and to interact with others using these skills. In games children also learn that knowing the rules increases their own chance of success, and that when they all follow the rules they have more fun. Social harmony comes when we all agree to the rules and choose to follow them. This structure gives us the chance to develop our own creative individuality, an important gift to bring to society.

Chapter 16

The world we live in

As parents and teachers we influence the future of the world. Today's children will be tomorrow's citizens and leaders. Parenting is the thread that connects yesterday, today, and tomorrow. The skills, values, and goals that you have and share with your children today, will live on in them and become a part of our future society. You will be involved in this society either as an active participant or as a retired observer, but today's children will become the leaders, the primary influences of our tomorrow. They will be making the decisions about health care and services to the elderly in the future. They will be practising their values and goals and passing them on to future generations. Your task today will influence the future of our world.

Allow childhood to be a protective caring time, a learning time, a time when the child can develop the talents and skills necessary to become a responsible adult in a world that values freedom, human dignity, individual responsibility, equality, and concern for each other. Those future possibilities will be greatly influenced by your everyday relationships and responses to your children. The relationships that they have with you will be the pattern for their future relationships. Human personalities seek out what is familiar and will bring about new relationships and situations that they have previously learned to be a part of. The experiences of childhood stay with us throughout our life.

It is human nature to seek the emotional state that is familiar to us. What is experienced and thereby learned from the environment in the early years sets up lifetime patterns. What happens at home each day, in school each day, and in other daily activities all influence how we live our lives. All things matter.

Seeking values

If reason, caring, respect, consideration and cooperation have been the basis of your family life, that is what your children are most likely to seek out in their adult relationships. If control, disregard for each other, contempt and ridicule dominate in your family, they are likely to seek that too. Think about what you value, what is healthy and then work toward providing your children with the basis for that.

Our goal of parenting for a healthy future is best met when we are aware that each of us has a separate, individual self. We each have our own thoughts, our own feelings, and our own activities. We each need to use our own thinking to direct our own activities. We each need to think for ourselves, use our own thinking to direct our own actions. That does not mean that we will not help each other or teach each other. It does mean that we will use words to give each other information or suggestions without expecting robot compliance.

When you follow another's directions without thinking about them yourself or understanding why you are doing them, they are not your actions. Someone else's head is thinking for your body. Then when your "thinker" is not with you to tell you what to do you will be at a loss as to what to do, you will be vulnerable to being directed and influenced by others. That is not part of being a free, healthy responsible person.

We are not here just to please others, impress others, or compete against others. Our task in life is to allow our individual talent to unfold and to live in harmony with others. Our sense of self grows as we experience achievements that have real meaning for society.

> Self perfection is by no means self seeking, for the imperfect man is an imperfect servant of the world and of humanity. The more perfect a man is the better does he serve the world. If the rose adorns itself, it adorns the garden.*

Becoming aware

The more aware of ourselves that we are, the better chance we have

*Steiner, Rudolf. *Knowledge of Higher Worlds and Its Attainment.* Anthroposophical Press, New York, 1947. Third Edition p175.

of meeting the individuality of others. As we get to know our own self and the individual self in others we become aware that there is a great deal to know beyond our usual daily affairs. When we develop within ourselves the awareness that there is something grander and wiser than ourselves and we strive to know about that, then we can find the strength to evolve to something higher. We can leave behind our desire to be the best, to be number one, and instead strive to build up our talents so that we can then bring them as gifts to the world.

When children have lived with parents who are balanced and are striving to grow in humanness they will have a life pattern for their own adult life. These are not qualities we can expect of children but a goal we strive for ourselves and thereby provide a model for their later years.

It is a very different thing when we strive *to do* the thing rather than striving *to be* right. Needing to be right and the best easily leads to arrogance. When we teach to others what we know it is given as a gift to the world. When we withhold what we know and try to control what others are thinking or doing we take away from them their rightful place in the world.

The role of the parent or teacher is not to rule and reject but to guide through understanding, teaching, and representing what is true, good, and beautiful. It is not to ignore, discount, disregard or criticize but to connect, care and protect; to know that everything and every moment matters. We do not want to relate to children with either dominance or permissiveness. Rather, we strive to bring conscious presence, awareness, and concern for the well being of the child as an individual and help her develop the skills needed to be a part of a social group.

Dominance is a reality in the animal world. Disinterest and lack of feeling are realities in the mechanical world. Neither are qualities that enhance humanness. When we value humans more than we do the machines that they have made, perhaps we will allow ourselves to open the windows to enjoy the fresh air rather than keeping all the windows closed because it is not good for the air conditioner for the windows to be opened! Perhaps we will then be able to put in perspective the medical technology news that "the mechanical heart operated successfully, but the patient died."

Human Qualities

Understanding, caring, and love are qualities that we will strive for to bring humanness to our children and to the world that they are growing in to. Understanding, caring, love and kindness come from the heart and can be seen in the eyes of those who care. **Take time to enjoy your children,** and find words to express your joy to them. Remember hugs often convey a message that words miss. A parent's greatest gift to his or her child is to help her develop a healthy personality. Then she will be able to meet life's challenges, and make free choices based on personal values of what is right for herself and the world, not choices based on other people's "shoulds". A person who feels that they are able to handle whatever comes to them in life has an inner strength that is a tremendous gift. Much of what happens to us in this world is beyond our control, but our attitudes toward what happens and how we respond to it is what we can control.

Help your children develop the human qualities of caring for others and things, patience, integrity, consideration, cooperation, respect for others and themselves, responsibility, and self reliance — which is not be to confused with independence. None of us can ever be independent of others, our lives are intertwined in a complex weaving that provides us with the daily essentials of living. We want to help children develop the skills they will need to provide for themselves as much as possible still realizing there will be times when they will count on the talents and skills of others.

Allow children to experience reverence and wonder at the good and the beautiful. Help them to be aware of what is around them so that they can live life as fully human beings. By developing our human qualities we can find new ways of relating to each other, grow beyond the dominance and submission of the animal world, and free ourselves to be truly human. By realizing that humans can go beyond dominance and submission (traits that are appropriate for the animal world) we can then learn to allow for each other's individual differences and meet each other in a new and wonderful way.

Honouring Others

There is room for each of us in this world and we need to be willing to allow it. Disagreements and conflicts are inevitable in life, we cannot expect to eliminate them but we can expect to listen to each other and use reason to resolve them and restore harmony. Healthy families acknowledge conflicts as inevitable and find ways to resolve them.

When people respect each other and allow for each other's individuality and personal space they create a reservoir of good will between them, a very valuable family space. Then when differences arise each can dip in to this reservoir of good will to resolve their differences. Morality depends on feelings and our ability to take an interest in our fellow man even when they have different beliefs and values. Morality cannot be forced, it is an inner experience and has to be allowed to grow. To be meaningful, personal values have to be freely chosen. Inner virtues are of more ultimate value to society than submission and obedience to commands, but it does take time to develop them. Inner values are the basis of personal responsibilities.

Without personal ethics we need laws, the less morality there is the more laws we need. Without personal values and ethics man's cleverness thinks up new ways to get around the laws, and then more laws are needed. When we understand the true nature of man and value living in harmony with each other, then we will strive to meet human needs and allow people to unfold their humanness.

When as parents we remain aware of our humanness and share that awareness in our family relationships we live life in the most honourable way. The task is challenging, and the rewards are great. Care for yourself, care for each other and care for the earth. Remember to grow.

Bibliography

Dorothy Corkille Briggs   *Your Child's Self Esteem*, Doubleday & Co., New York, 1970

Erik H Erikson   *Childhood and Society*, W. W. Norton and Co., New York, 1963

Raymond N Guarendi   *You're a Better Parent Than You Think!* Prentice Hall, New Jersey, 1985

Georg Kuhlewind   *From Normal to Healthy*, Lindisfarne Press, Maine, 1988

John Saxe   *The Blind Men and the Elephant*, McGraw Publishing, New York, 1963

Benjamin Spock   *Baby and Child Care*, Simon and Schuster, New York, 1976

Rudolf Steiner   *A Modern Art of Education*, Rudolf Steiner Press, London, 1972

Rudolf Steiner   *Knowledge of Higher Worlds and Its Attainment*, Anthroposophic Press, New York, 1964

Rudolf Steiner   *The Philosophy of Freedom*, Anthroposophic Press, New York, 1964

J. B. Watson   *Psychological Care of Infant and Child*, W. W. Norton and Co., New York, 1928

Helpful References

Virginia Axline   *Dibs in Search of Self,* Houghton Miflin, Boston, 1964

Rahima Baldwin   *You Are Your Child's First Teacher,* Celestial Arts, Berkely, 1988

Dotty Coplen   *Parenting a Path Through Childhood,* Floris Books, Edinburgh, 1982

Adel Faber & Elaine Mazlish   *How to Talk so Kids Will Listen & Listen So Kids Will Talk,* Avon Books, New York, 1982

Erich Fromm   *The Art of Loving,* Harper and Brothers, New York, 1956

Benjamin Hoff   *The TAO of Pooh,* Dutton, New York, 1982

Alfie Kohn   *No Contest – The Case Against Competition,* Houghton Miflin, Boston, 1986

Abraham Maslow   *Towards a Psychology of Being,* Van Nostrand, New York, 1962

Grace Mitchell   *A Very Practical Guide to Discipline with Young Children,* Telshare Publishing, Massachusetts, 1982

Gerald Nelson   *The One Minute Scolding,* Shambala, Colorado, 1984

Trina Paulus   *Hope For the Flowers,* Paulist Press, New York, 1972

Carl Rogers   *On Becoming a Person,* Houghton Miflin, Boston, 1961

Jean Salter   *The Incarnating Child,* Hawthorn Press, Stroud, 1987

Parenting a Path
through Childhood

Dotty Turner Coplen

Combining her experience as a mother and grandmother with her studies in psychology and social work, the author presents a warm and human way of understanding the nature and needs of children.

Parents and professionals working with children will find this a helpful book for understanding the needs of children, developing an awareness of their individual differences and observing how behaviour is learned.

Understanding parenting by thinking about 'Who' is a child, 'What' is a parent and brings the reader to the reality of daily living; ready to accept the child's unique individuality and to help him learn the art of living.

Floris Books, Edinburgh

Other Books from Hawthorn Press

ALL YEAR ROUND
Ann Druitt, Christine Fynes-Clinton, Marÿe Rowling.

Brimming with seasonal stories, activities, crafts, poems and recipes, this book offers an inspirational guide to celebrating festivals throughout the seasons. A sequel to *The Children's Year*, this book arises from the festivals workshops run by the authors at the annual *Lifeways* conference at Emerson College.

"The words are ours, the festivals are yours." This book encourages both adults and children to explore forgotten corners of the educational curriculum and to develop and adapt the various festivals to fit their own family traditions. The enthusiasm and colourful creativity with which this book is written is guaranteed to stimulate interest in the diverse and multiple joys of the seasons.

200 x 250mm; 288pp approx; limpbound; colour cover; fully illustrated ISBN 1 869 890 47 7

BETWEEN FORM AND FREEDOM
A PRACTICAL GUIDE TO THE TEENAGE YEARS
Betty Staley.

Betty Staley offers a wealth of insights about teenagers, providing a compassionate, intelligent and intuitive look into the minds of children and adolescents. She explores the nature of adolescence and looks at teenagers' needs in relation to family, friends, schools, love and the arts. Issues concerning stress, depression, drug and alcohol abuse and eating disorders are included.

210 x 135mm; 288pp; sewn limp bound; illustrations
ISBN 1 869 890 08 6

CHILDRENS YEAR
CRAFT AND CLOTHES FOR CHILDREN AND PARENTS TO MAKE
Stephanie Cooper, Christine Fynes-Clinton and Marÿe Rowling.
You needn't be an experienced craftsperson to create beautiful things! This charmingly illustrated book encourages children and adults to try all sorts of different handwork, with different projects relating to the seasons of the year. Over 100 potential treasures are described, including toys and games from all sorts of natural materials, decorations and even children's clothes.
200 x 250mm; 220pp; illustrated; sewn limp bound; ISBN 1 869 890 00 0

CHILDS PLAY 3
GAMES FOR LIFE FOR CHILDREN AND TEENAGERS
Wil van Haren and Rudolf Kischnick
Translated by Plym Peters and Tony Langham
A tried and tested games book consisting of numerous ideas for running races, duels, wrestling matches, activity and ball games of skill and agility. Its clear lay-out, detailed explanations and diagrams and its indexing of games by age suitability and title makes *Child's Play* an invaluable and enjoyable resource book for parents, teachers and play leaders.
October 1994; 215 x 145mm; 128pp paperback; colour cover; ISBN 1 869 890 63 9

FESTIVALS, FAMILY AND FOOD
Diana Carey and Judy Large.
A ideal companion to *Festivals Together,* this explores those numerous annual 'feast days' which children love celebrating. It was written in response to children and busy parents asking, "What can we do at Christmas and Easter?
What games can we play? What can we make?"
Packed full of ideas on things to do, food to make, songs to sing and games to play, it's an invaluable resources book designed to help you and your family celebrate the various festival days scattered round the year.
                                                                    The Observer
200 x 250mm; 216pp; limp bound; colour cover; fully illustrated; ISBN 0 950 706 23 X

FESTIVALS TOGETHER
A GUIDE TO MULTI-CULTURAL CELEBRATION
Sue Fitzjohn, Minda Weston, Judy Large

This is a resource guide for celebration, and for observing special days according to traditions based on many cultures. It brings together the experience, sharing and activities of individuals from multi-faith communities all over the world – Buddhist, Christian, Hindu, Jewish, Muslim and Sikh. Its unifying thread is our need for meaning, for continuity and for joy. Written with parents and teachers in mind, it will be of use to every school and family. Richly illustrated, there is a four page insert of seasonal prints by John Gibbs for your wall.

200 x 250mm; 224pp; limp bound; colour cover; fully illustrated; ISBN 1 869 890 46 9

THE INCARNATING CHILD
Joan Salter.

"Our birth is but a sleep and a forgetting;" Joan Salter picks up Wordsworth's theme and follows the soul life of tiny babies into childhood and adolescence. A specialist in maternal and child care, she addresses physical, spiritual and psychological development as well as environmental factors. This book will be particularly valuable for those embarking on parenthood for the first time.

210 x 135mm; 224pp; sewn limp bound; illustrations and photographs;
ISBN 1 869 890 04 3

LIFEWAYS
WORKING WITH FAMILY QUESTIONS
Gudrun Davy and Bons Voors

Lifeways is about children, about family life and about being a
parent. But above all it is about freedom, and how the tension
between family life and personal fulfilment can be resolved.
*These essays affirm that creating a family, even if you are a father on your
own, or a working mother, can be a joyful, positive and spiritual work.
The first essay is one of the wisest and most balanced discussions of
women's rôles I have read.*
Fiona Handley, Church of England Newspaper.

150mm x 210mm; 328pp; sewn limp bound; ISBN 0 950 706 24 8

THE OTHER WISE MAN
Henry Van Dyck.

Adapted by Gabriel Bradford Millar.

*"You know the story of the three Wise Men who came from the East to
offer their gifts at the manger in Bethlehem. But have you heard the story
of the fourth Wise Man who also saw the Star and set out to follow it?
Artaban did not arrive with the other three to honour the Child Jesus, but
his was a long, strange journey in search of a King."*
Beautifully illustrated by Terry Thomas, this is a classic fireside
reader; a story sure to become an annual family tradition at
Epiphany.

216 x 138mm; 64pp; colour cover;
ISBN 1 869 890 66 3

TO A DIFFERENT DRUMBEAT
A PRACTICAL GUIDE TO PARENTING CHILDREN WITH SPECIAL NEEDS

Paddy Clarke, Holly Kofsky and Jenni Lauruol.

This is a book which aims to enhance the process of caring for children who have special needs. In an age dominated by illusions of perfection and an increasing reliance on medical intervention, the message here is a bold one: "Look what we can do. See how life and society are richer through diversity, and how much we can learn from our children"

246 x 189mm; 240pp; sewn limp bound; illustrations;
ISBN 1 869 890 09 4

VOYAGE THROUGH CHILDHOOD INTO THE ADULT WORLD
A GUIDE TO CHILD DEVELOPMENT

Eva A Frommer

Human beings have a long infancy during which they are dependent upon others for the means of life and growth – such a book on child development is therefore vital. Many of Frommer's ideas in this book derive from her professional observations as a child psychiatrist and include her personal distillations of Rudolf Steiner's teachings. A deep concern for the uniqueness of each individual child permeates this book, while offering practical solutions to the challenges of raising a child at each stage of his or her development.

October 1994; 216 x 138mm; 140pp approx; paperback; colour and black & white photographs; ISBN 1 869 890 59 0

ORDERS

If you have difficulty ordering from a bookshp, please order direct from:
Hawthorn Press,
Hawthorn House,
1 Lansdown Lane, Stroud GL5 1BJ UK
Telephone: 01453 757040   Fax: 01453 751138